TWAYNE'S WORLD AUTHORS SERIES

A Survey of the World's Literature

Sylvia E. Bowman, Indiana University
GENERAL EDITOR

GERMANY

Ulrich Weisstein, Indiana University
EDITOR

Joseph von Eichendorff

(TWAS 163)

TWAYNE'S WORLD AUTHORS SERIES (TWAS)

The purpose of TWAS is to survey the major writers—novelists, dramatists, historians, poets, philosophers, and critics—of the nations of the world. Among the national literatures covered are those of Australia, Canada, China, Eastern Europe, France, Germany, Greece, India, Italy, Japan, Latin America, New Zealand, Poland, Russia, Scandinavia, Spain, and the African nations, as well as Hebrew, Yiddish, and Latin Classical literatures. This survey is complemented by Twayne's United States Authors Series and English Authors Series.

The intent of each volume in these series is to present a critical-analytical study of the works of the writer; to include biographical and historical material that may be necessary for understanding, appreciation, and critical appraisal of the writer; and to present all material in clear, concise English—but not to vitiate the scholarly content of the work by doing so.

Joseph von Eichendorff

By EGON SCHWARZ, 1922-

Washington University

Twayne Publishers, Inc.   ::   New York

Preface

Writing an introduction to Joseph von Eichendorff for an English-speaking public entails certain advantages and disadvantages. Since Eichendorff is virtually unknown in the Anglo-American world, the literary historian can safely ignore the entire legendary and folkloristic growth that has enveloped the author and his works in the century following his death. He does not have to waste time in clarifying the term *Heimatdichter,* an expression overladen with unfortunate emotional overtones, which is only inadequately and misleadingly translated as "regional poet." The fact that Eichendorff was born into the landed gentry of Silesia and was influenced, throughout his career as a writer, by the values he absorbed from his native landscape and society, is of purely informative, and not of ideological, significance outside of Germany. Similarly, his Catholicism, both as a religious force and as a vehicle for his cultural polemics, is unlikely to arouse controversy anywhere except in his native land, where political or confessional propaganda all too often appears under the guise of literary criticism. It would also prove unfruitful in England or America to split hairs over the exact degree to which a German writer is involved with the Romantic movement. While it has been a favorite pastime of German literary historians to draw learned and exceedingly subtle distinctions between Storm and Stress, Classicism, Old, Young, and Post-Romantics, from a European or comparative point of view the entire panorama of the age of Goethe and large portions of German nineteenth century literature appear as arch-Romantic, with Eichendorff, in so far as he is perceived at all, being a most typical proponent of the movement. Thus, a lengthy disquisition on Eichendorff's qualities as a Late Romantic and on those elements of his spiritual makeup that connected him with the *Biedermeier,* would hardly elicit great interest.

Finally, there would be no point in insisting on the sentimental ingredients of Eichendorff's view of nature as a mythical embodiment of the German landscape and on the resemblance some of his protagonists may bear to archetypes of the German national character: dreamy, carefree, apolitical, sunny-hearted singers and fiddlers wandering through their native hills, dales, and forests.[1] The sober foreigner who has experienced the Germans in a different historical role and who has noticed, in their country, the signals of an industrialization which has all but devoured the once extensive forests, no matter how German, would remain incredulous and untouched by such a presentation. In short, the advantages to be gained from creating an English rather than a German Eichendorff consist in the opportunity to discard some of the timeworn clichés that have accumulated around his figure and to penetrate to the core of his poetic substance, valid in a broad context of time and space.

But this is precisely where the difficulties begin. Stripped of mythology, Eichendorff's strength lies in his poems, but not so much in their subject matter or ideational content as in their rhythms and melodies, their ornaments and images; in other words: in exactly those intimate features of language that are ultimately untranslatable. Important poetic works in the German tongue, for example, some of Rilke's, have been successfully rendered in English and other languages. This is partly due, of course, to the international character assumed, in modern times, by cultural and literary phenomena. It is also due to the highly intellectual and topical content of Rilke's poetry. Eichendorff's poems, on the other hand, have largely remained untranslated. They belong to a different tradition of poetry in which the musical, acoustic, and emotive faculties of language are exploited, often to the detriment of its semantic or thought properties. The German *Lied* is the glory of this lyrical tradition, and Eichendorff figures prominently, together with Goethe, Brentano, Mörike, and a mere handful of others, as having contributed to the perfection of the genre.

If the *Lied*-like poem requires a supplement or modification to become accessible outside of its native linguistic environment, it is not so much translation (which is at best an insufficient guide to its principal values) as setting to music. And this is indeed the manner in which Eichendorff has transcended the narrow confines of his nationality and his craft. Some of his *Lieder* have attained the anonymity of folk song, and the musical compositions based on them can be said to be the property of music lovers all over the world. Pleasing as this may be, it should not obscure the fact that the explication of untranslatable poetry is a feat hard to perform. I shall try to solve the problem, wherever examples are necessary, by juxtaposing original passages of poetry with transliterations which will attempt to bring out the points in question rather than aiming for poetic values in their own right. (The same will hold true for my prose translations.) Let us remember that translations, like women, are either beautiful or faithful! But with all the good will on the part of the reader taken for granted, it is quite obvious that in the lyrical sphere, probably of central significance for our poet, a series of approximations will have to serve for full attainment.

Next in importance for Eichendorff's claim to literary greatness are his short tales, often called *novellas* in commemoration of the genre's origins in the Italian Renaissance. Although a master in this craft for much the same lyrical reasons as in poetry, Eichendorff has been able to exploit the momentum inherent in the narrative style to produce universally comprehensible effects, particularly in his immortal *Aus dem Leben eines Taugenichts,* one of the most successful actualizations of the form existing in world literature. The task of demonstrating Eichendorff's sophisticated and versatile craftsmanship in this art form should not present insurmountable difficulties.

A discussion of Joseph von Eichendorff as a novelist presents obstacles of a different kind. In the form of the short novel or novella, German writers were past masters and among the world's leaders, whereas there are few great full-length novels in the history of nineteenth-century German literature. This is not the place to offer conjectures as to how this state of affairs came about. Suffice it to say that, while indispensable for an understanding of the poet and characteristic enough of German Romantic prose, Eichendorff's two long novels are situated somewhat apart from the European mainstream and must remain, from an international point of view, eccentric curiosa without having a significant function in the historical development of the genre. By revealing the inner dynamics of Eichendorff's main novel, *Ahnung und Gegenwart,* and relating it to the author's *idearium,*

I shall attempt to establish its significance in a nonhistorical context.

No attempt will be made to resurrect Eichendorff's dramatic works, some of which, according to one of the most knowledgeable and perceptive scholars, were stillborn children of his muse.[2] Eichendorff was more important as a translator of Spanish literature than as a dramatist. Especially his masterful rendering of Calderón's *Great Theater of the World* commands admiration to this very day, when the competition has grown considerably. But it is too delicate a matter to evaluate a writer's translations from one language into another for the readers of a third, nor is it essential for the purpose of providing a first glance into his poetic world. Likewise, it will scarcely be possible to give much space to a discussion of Eichendorff's endeavors as an essayist writing about cultural, literary, and historical subjects. It is in this area that Eichendorff's religious and philosophical orientations are most clearly perceived, but they are today of a more specialized interest. Instead, by selecting for interpretation some representative and artistically meaningful works in prose and poetry, we shall attempt to characterize his craft so as to help the interested reader to gain an understanding of a writer remote from his own cultural sphere and to enable him to penetrate more deeply into Eichendorff's poetic world on his own, if he should so desire.

Thus the aim of this book is twofold: to introduce the English-speaking reader to some central aspects of Joseph von Eichendorff's art and, at the same time, while dispensing with some of the prevailing pieties, to point out those features of his work that seem most enduring in the nonparochial perspective of world literature.

Profoundly indebted to a great number of excellent Eichendorff scholars, the author of the present monograph has thought it preferable to limit direct source references to concrete cases such as quotations. A list of the scholarly works that were especially instrumental in shaping his thought is contained in the appended bibliography.

E. S.

Acknowledgments

This book owes much of its existence to the generous support lent to me by Washington University in the form of a leave of absence and various subsidies. Thanks are also due to the *Journal of English and Germanic Philology* for permitting me to reprint, in English translation, an old article of mine which had appeared there in 1957, "Bemerkungen zu Eichendorff's Erzähltechnik."[1] Similarly, I am indebted to the French journal *Etudes Germaniques* for permission to recast my article "Der Taugenichts zwischen Heimat und Exil" (1957)[2] and to the New York publishing house McGraw-Hill for allowing me to translate and reprint the postscript to my 1969 edition of *Aus dem Leben eines Taugenichts*,[3] which, in turn, was based on the *Etudes Germaniques* essay. I am grateful to my colleague Herbert Lindenberger for reading the manuscript and making valuable suggestions and to my wife for her repeated proof-reading efforts. Sylvia Holste-Lilie helped me most efficiently with problems of translation. Perhaps I should also thank my wife and my children for giving me the pretext of claiming that without them the book would have been finished several years ago.

Contents

Chronology

1846-47 Translation of Calderón's *Autos Sacramentales I*
1853 Translation of Calderón's *Autos Sacramentales II*
1855 Wife's death
1857 The poet dies

CHAPTER 1

Biographical Facts and Their Influence on Eichendorff's Development

TO those who insist on a close correlation between the life and the works of a writer, Eichendorff presents something of a puzzle. His performance as a punctilious government official, faithful husband, and loving father does not seem to have any connection with the carefree, unattached characters of his fiction whose perpetual migrations their sedentary creator never ceased to extol as a moral virtue. Conversely, he relentlessly condemned those devoted but pitiable souls who, like himself, spent their lives bent over reams of petitions and reports.

A glance at some of the other German Romantics indeed reveals a different pattern. They are either esoteric youths alternating between ecstatic and angelic states of mind, and destined to die an early death, like Wackenroder and Novalis; or the anti-bourgeois and utterly Bohemian types with torn souls, like Clemens Brentano and E. T. A. Hoffmann, whose own lives seem to have been the foremost models for their artistic creations. In contrast to this, Eichendorff seems to have been an armchair romantic whose civilian existence was strangely dissociated from the figments of his imagination. To be sure, he is not the only member of the German Romantic school to exhibit such a dichotomy between life and mind. Ludwig Tieck was another, and so was Friedrich Schlegel. But Tieck underwent many changes in his life and to each phase in his development there corresponds a concomitant shift in style, subject matter, and intellectual posture, whereas Schlegel, as the theoretician, philosopher, and historian of the movement does not provoke such comparisons between his biographical and creative systems. In Eichendorff's case, however, there is and remains the curious contrast between an exemplary middle-class life and the typically romantic out-of-doors existence that he unwaveringly advocated with the zeal and gusto of one who has experienced it. And so he has in a very specific sense.

During his entire life Eichendorff remained oriented toward his childhood and early youth. Early experiences and impressions play an important role in most people's lives, but the intensity with which Eichendorff's mind kept returning to the locale of his origins and exploring its topography in work after work is rare. Since the scenes were enacted in the theater of his childhood that constitute the repertory of his poetic works, it will be necessary to recapture them as much as possible.

Joseph von Eichendorff was born into the landed gentry of Upper Silesia on March 10, 1788. Though annexed by Prussia in the Seven Years' War a quarter of a century earlier, his native province was still very Austrian and Catholic in character, complete with its manner of speaking, its orientation toward Vienna, and the informal mingling of Slavs and Germans. Eichendorff's birthplace was Schloss Lubowitz, a castle very much like the countless ones that he conjured up in his prose and poetry. The harmonious, almost idyllic life of his early years with the frequent hunting parties and other gay festivities, incessant visits to and from the neighboring castles, the castle itself with its ancient furniture and musical clocks, and in particular the Rococo gardens[1] with their hedges and mythological statues, tree-lined alleys, colorful flowers, murmuring fountains and, most importantly perhaps, the surrounding boundless forests constitutes not only the scenery of Eichendorff's childhood but also that of a majority of his stories and poems.

One of Eichendorff's most perceptive biographers, Paul Stöcklein, ventures the opinion[2] that in this locale the poet underwent two separate "Urerlebnisse," early, archetypal experiences that retained their vigor as formative influences throughout his life. The first of these was poetry, which came to young Joseph in the guise of both Polish and German folk songs, fairy tales, and medieval legends, as well as in an early impulse, welling up from within, to produce the like, resulting in childlike poems on the persons and the nature surrounding him. The other experience was religion. From a friendly chaplain the child learned biblical stories, whose deep emotional impact, was never to be supplanted by his future studies. The orthodox, almost political Catholicism of the older man had its origins in these early sentimental encounters with the imagery of the Bible. More than once Eichendorff described these twin influences in his fiction, for example in the autobiographical reminiscences of Friedrich, the central character in the novel *Ahnung und Gegenwart*.[3]

It would be too schematic to suggest a crass conflict between these two forces working on Eichendorff's youthful soul. After all, they both sprang from his poetic imagination and, furthermore, they even entered an explicit intellectual reconciliation during his university years, in the Romantic doctrines of Eichendorff's teacher Joseph Görres, and yet there exist undeniable tensions between Eichendorff's conception of poetry and his religious faith. What is more, these tensions lend his creative work a vibrating energy without which it would be lacking an important dimension. Reduced to the simplest terms, the reason for the lack of total compatibility between his two formative influences lies in the role played by "nature" in each of them. For the poet, nature, objectified in the forests, streams, and mountains, but also in man's inner impulses broadly identifiable as erotic, is a vital force of inspiration. Nostalgia for an existence in harmony with this power is every man's lot, and it is the urge to give adequate expression to this longing which makes a poet out of him. "Schläft ein Lied in allen Dingen"—(A song slumbers in all things)[4]—this often-quoted line testifies to Eichendorff's belief that poetry is embedded in all things, being the essence of the individuations of nature. This is a pantheistic thought. And the conclusion of the four-line poem "Wünschelrute" (Divining Rod) from which it is taken—"Und die Welt hebt an zu singen/ Triffst du nur das Zauberwort" (And the world begins to sing/ If only you find the magic word)—is an appeal to a witchcraft which is not easily reconciled with the simple Christianity Eichendorff advocated at other times.

A recurrent image in Eichendorff's fiction and poetry aptly demonstrates the difficulty. It is the allegory of nature at its loveliest, Spring, personified as a minstrel who lures the unwary, susceptible youth into the Mountain of Venus, the abode of all sensuous pleasures. Without experiencing them he would remain unresponsive to the concrete beauties of the world, which are the nourishment of poetry. But the Spring allegory also contains elements of religious objection raised by Christianity against such nature worship. In the Christian world view, nature is a danger and a threat. Man is not only a vegetative but also a moral being, with a soul and an inborn quest for immortality. By giving in to his longing for union with nature, without which the poet can neither live nor create, he falls under its spell and becomes himself subject to its endless rhythm of blooming and wilting, alertness and torpor, revival and death. Only religion can interrupt the cycle and give life an aim and a purpose; only the Christian faith promises immortality. It is easy to see why so many of Eichendorff's characters are torn between earthly and heavenly love, and to understand the reasons for the allegorical embodiment of these opposing tendencies in Venus and Mary, the Queens of Earth and Heaven. No matter what plot, what imagery, what ideological superstructure Eichendorff invents to reconcile these longings within him, there always remains in his works a poetically fruitful tension between the love of the earth and the love of Christ.

A third force which can ultimately be traced to his childhood experiences is active in Eichendorff, a force which he did not so much express in his writings, but one which all the more fashioned his personal life. The happy marriage of his parents, who were surrounded by a gay circle of children, his father's regular and satisfying occupation as a country squire living close to the soil, were values which Eichendorff absorbed in his most impressionable years. He must have incorporated these beneficial influences into his personality long before he became intellectually conscious of their existence, and when the time was ripe he in turn became an exemplary family man. It is not too farfetched to suggest that the ideal harmony in his social sphere must have conflicted, at some level of his subconscious, with the demands of both poetry and religion. For the poet should be unencumbered by the tribulations and obligations arising from the struggle for an economic existence, and the *homo religiosus* must turn his back on the joys of this earth. In many a poem and prose passage Eichendorff described this dilemma without solution, most impressively perhaps in the sonnet that serves to introduce the section "Sängerleben" (Life of the Poet) in his collected works, whose very title "Schlimme Wahl" (Evil Choice)[5] expresses the lack of viable alternatives:

Du sahst die Fei ihr goldnes Haar sich strählen,
Wenn morgens früh noch alle Wälder schweigen,
Gar viele da im Feldgrund sich versteigen,
Und weiss doch keiner, wen sie wird erwählen.

Von einer andern Dam' hört ich erzählen
Im platten Land, die Bauern rings dir zeigen
Ihr Schloss, Park, Weiler—alles ist dein eigen,
Freist du das Weib—wer möcht' im Wald sich quälen!

Sie werden dich auf einen Phaeton heben,
Das Hochzeitscarmen tönt, es blinkt die Flasche,
Weitrauschend hinterdrein viel vornehm Wesen.

Doch streift beim Zug dich aus dem Walde eben
Der Feie Blick, und brennt dich nicht zu Asche:
Fahr wohl, bist nimmer ein Poet gewesen!

You saw the fairy comb her golden hair
Early in the morning when the woods are quiet,
And many lose their way in her wild domain
And yet nobody knows whom she will choose.

I heard tell of another lady
In the flatlands; there the peasants show you
Her castle, park and hamlet—all this is yours
If you wed her—Who wants to brood in the forest?

They will lift you onto a phaeton,
The nuptial poem is intoned, the bottle sparkles,
Many a genteel creature belongs to her rustling retinue.

But if from the forest the fairy's eye grazes you
As you pass and you do not burn to ashes:
Farewell, you have never been a poet!

In this particular context, the poem hardly requires an interpretation. It helps one to comprehend more readily why Eichendorff never tired of positing the two unsatisfactory alternatives always facing his youthful protagonists: domestication with its concomitant loss of poetic élan and bohemian license with the accompanying loss of self. It is hardly an accident that the courtly code of the chivalric age, to which Eichendorff was so deeply indebted in his outlook, should provide two quasi-technical terms for these alternatives: *sich verligen* and *sich verliesen*, to stagnate and to lose oneself to the world. There is no way out of the quandary, except perhaps through the individual's unquestioning submission to divine guidance.[6]

To complete the picture of the formative events in Eichendorff's childhood, one must not neglect the French Revolution. To be sure, it broke out the year after Joseph's birth and had run its course before he became conscious of history. But Silesia was remote from its scene, and it took many years before its pervading and disrupting influences were felt among the aristocratic families who made up Eichendorff's circle. Everything in his mature spiritual makeup, his Romantic philosophy of life, his political and religious conservatism, his family loyalty, class consciousness, and economic interests, conspired to make him an opponent of the Revolution. Still, the attitude expressed in his writings is not completely free of a certain ambiguity,[7] and complicated as the relationship may be, it is possible to link up the impression this historical movement must have made on his sensitive mind with certain unresolved ambivalences in Eichendorff's poetic *idearium*.

As is the case with so many writers, on the most profound level the tone of all of Eichendorff's writings is characterized by a longing for "die schöne alte Zeit," an expression too nostalgic and poetic to be adequately rendered by the literal translation "the good old days." What is implied by these words is a desire to return to the idyllic harmony of childhood, a desire which is so permeated with the knowledge of its own futility that it becomes a true "recherche du temps perdu" the frustration of which is only mitigated by its religious overtones. This nostalgia is thus not only an abstract mental process, as it would probably remain with most people, but in Eichendorff's mind it is endowed with very concrete features, "spatialized" in the scenery of his native castle with its beautiful Rococo gardens and personified in the characters who populated the world of his childhood. With one half of his mind, the poet understood that much of his poetic inspiration emanated from these emotion-laden images.

Since Eichendorff was not only an emotional but also a rational being, he was not satisfied with attributing the loss of this early paradise to the mere dwindling of childhood but also sought for an intellectual explanation which would do justice to the moral, political, and sociological ramifications of the problem. There is evidence that he attributed the disintegration and gradual disappearance of his aristocratic world to the French Revolution or at least to the forces which brought it about. Had Eichendorff been an undiluted, unadulterated Romantic, his vision of a paradisiac past would have remained his chief source of inspiration and, as a consequence, his poetry would exhibit a much more sentimental and unified character, even if to the detriment of ambiguity, differentiation, and interest. But with the other, more rational half of his being, he rejected this infatuation with the past as *reactionary*.

Eichendorff has often been described as a joyous, optimistic, and unsentimentally virile person, someone the Germans like to describe, with an alliterative cliché, as "frisch fröhlich frei." It is this side of his personality, affirmatively oriented toward the present and the future, that reacted against the emotional cult of a mythical past in which the Romantic movement indulged. It enabled him to enlist religion on the side of sober, optimistic realism. Thus we gain a glimpse of yet another aspect of the poet's fundamental allegory. Venus and her pagan entourage are associated with the old order, with nature worship and its inescapable rhythm of revival and petrification. Christianity, in contrast, is the modern force, allowing man to be a moral being capable of clear judgment and social criticism. It would be an exaggeration to say that Eichendorff approved of or condoned the French Revolution even when viewing it from this pole of his temperament. But he did accuse the past, and especially his own social class, of having contributed to its own downfall. Concretely speaking, he charged the aristocracy with being morally responsible—be it through ignorance, infirmity, or neglect of their social obligations—for their own destruction. Out of these contradictions arises, philosophically speaking, a fruitful dialectic tension in Eichendorff's intellect and, from an esthetic point of view, a delightful poetic ambivalence which pervades his work and enhances its value.

Compared to the basic triad of Eichendorff's early experiences —aristocratic family life on a country estate, poetry, and religion— everything that followed his Lubowitz childhood could add little more than nuances to his outlook on life. The task that remains is,

therefore, to glance at the biographical facts and fit the individual pieces into the mosaic as chronology supplies them. Together with his brother who was only one year his senior, Joseph,
at the age of thirteen, was sent to the Catholic *Gymnasium* in
Breslau. The benefit of the four years there seems to have con-
sisted in the profusion of theatrical plays and music that was
provided for the students in the typical fashion of Catholic board-
ing schools of the day. Eichendorff first studied at Halle where
student life was rough and boisterous but not intellectually oriented. The termination of his two rather tumultuous student years
was marked by a trip to the Harz mountains and North Germany,
Eichendorff's one and only major foot journey, to which he reacted with the same boundless enthusiasm for nature and freedom
as do his fictional heroes. In later years, the family cares, the
duties of office, and the strictures of finance increasingly reduced
the radius of Eichendorff's peregrinations, preventing him even
from visiting his beloved brother who resided in Northern Italy.

As was the habit in Germany (largely preserved to this day),
the two Eichendorff brothers moved to another university after
two years. Joseph's expectations on moving to Heidelberg, an important center of cultural life, were fully rewarded. It was here
that he was exposed to the main intellectual currents of his era.
To be more precise, he was introduced to Romantic thought by
a young university lecturer, Joseph Görres. Görres, then in his
early thirties, was by all accounts a magnetic personality. Eichendorff was irresistibly drawn to him, and it must be regarded as
a fortuitous event for the development of his mind that the
older man responded to his admiration and accepted him into
his mental as well as personal intimacy.[8] This encounter was
more decisive than later meetings with such romantic celebrities
as Brentano, Arnim, Adam Müller, and Heinrich von Kleist, which
had more of a social than intellectual significance for Eichendorff. It is through Görres that the two forces which were
awakened in his childhood, that of a magic-poetical concept of
nature on the one hand and of the Christian faith on the other,
were amalgamated into a coherent whole. Paul Stöcklein goes so
far as to call this "the birth of his conscious, integrated personality and his poetry."[9] The tensions between these two worlds
have already been alluded to. Stöcklein further emphasizes that
the combination of these two forces, existing as separate im-

pulses in the eighteenth century, was made especially difficult intellectually because of a struggle between the new creed of nature and the petrified church orthodoxy.

Eichendorff's university study was followed by the customary "grand tour" which, in view of the brothers' pecuniary straits, turned out not to be too grand after all. But their travels did last for half a year and, while mainly confined to Germany, took them as far as Paris on one occasion. An attempt to devote themselves to agriculture as assistants to their father, in the hope of making it their future profession, had to be given up after two years because of the financial condition of the ancestral estates. In 1810 the inseparable brothers reluctantly traveled to Vienna, resolved to prepare themselves for careers as government officials. Studies for the civil service examinations, participation in the great capital's social activities, enjoyment of its unique theater life, and the writing of his first novel occupied young Eichendorff's Viennese days in frenzied alternation. His good fortune brought him into close contact with one of the great minds of the century and an initiator of European Romanticism, Friedrich Schlegel—a prolific writer and brilliant conservative, who had moved to the Austrian capital some years before to assume the position of Court Secretary in the Imperial Chancellory. The ties of friendship extended to Schlegel's intellectual wife Dorothea—Moses Mendelssohn's daughter—who encouraged Eichendorff in his ambitions to become a writer and sympathetically observed the growth of his first novel, composed largely in the year 1811. It was she who supplied the suggestive title *Ahnung und Gegenwart* (terms borrowed from her husband's public lectures) with which it entered the annals of literary history. The influence of the Schlegel household, which included Dorothea's son Philip Veit, a painter, can hardly be overestimated. Eichendorff also renewed his earlier acquaintance with Adam Müller, who had been brought to Vienna by the famous statesman Friedrich Gentz. Müller's conservative theories on society and the state did not remain without influence on Eichendorff's receptive mind, preconditioned as it was for such a view of the world by virtue of birth, upbringing, and religious faith.

Joseph von Eichendorff's pursuit of a professional career was luckless from the beginning. It has already been reported that his venture into gentleman farming got off to a bad start (and had to

be abandoned because of the imminent loss of the family possessions). In Vienna, in spite of passing the civil service examinations with flying colors in the year after his arrival, he was
unable to obtain employment. In 1813 he voluntarily enlisted
and intermittently served in the army until 1816. His opposition
to the Napoleonic occupation and his sense of German patriotism
are reflected in his writings, especially in *Ahnung und Gegenwart*, a novel containing many autobiographical elements. The
year before his discharge from the army he married his fiancée
of several years, Aloysia von Larisch, a young lady of the Silesian
aristocracy, the daughter of a neighboring family with a background identical to that of the Eichendorffs. Their marriage was
destined to be extremely happy, apparently without any cloud
on the horizon.

But Eichendorff's search for a career continued to be rather
unsuccessful. Finally in 1816, after his endeavors tò find a position in his beloved Austria had failed repeatedly, he obtained
poorly compensated employment as an official of the Silesian
provincial government in Breslau. It is characteristic of Eichendorff's ill fortune in professional matters that he was thirty-four
years of age and the father of four children before he received
his first reasonably comfortable salary as a Government Coun-
cillor in Danzig. The following year, 1822, also marked Eichendorff's total severance from his earlier existence. His mother died,
and the last of the Eichendorff's Silesian estates, the Lubowitz of
his birth which looms so large in his poetry, was irretrievably
lost. From this moment on, Eichendorff lived a retiring and completely unassuming life as a devoted government official, successively in Danzig, Königsberg, and Berlin, writing and publishing his novels, stories, and poems. There is much evidence
that, in spite of the meticulous fulfillment of his duties, he was
profoundly dissatisfied with his public occupation. His happiness
returned in the circle of his family and when he was sitting "at
his other desk,"[10] that of the poet. We have his testimony, however, that his job as a government official did not interfere with
his poetry. The two worlds existed in complete separation from
one another, and Eichendorff kept them hermetically apart.

In 1844 he quit the civil service, ostensibly for reasons of
health. A disagreement with his superior regarding the conduct
of Catholic church and school affairs—the section dealing with

these questions had been entrusted to him in the Prussian Ministry of Culture—may have been the actual cause for his retirement at the age of 56.[11] But this break had been prepared for years by the mounting incompatibility of Eichendorff's temperament with the demands of paperwork and government administration—activities which he ceaselessly attacked and derided in his literary works. From 1844 on, supported by a small pension, Joseph von Eichendorff was free to devote himself exclusively to the two concerns so dear to his heart: his family and his writing. In 1857, two years after the death of his wife, the poet died, not quite seventy years old, in the house of his daughter Therese in the city of Neisse.

CHAPTER 2

The Novelist

EICHENDORFF'S second full-length novel, *Dichter und ihre Gesellen* (the title is somewhat ambiguous since it can mean "Poets and their fellows, companions, or apprentices"), appeared in 1834, almost two decades after the first. In many ways it is a more controlled, more unified work of art, clearly a job of the mature craftsman and *routinier* of novel writing. It is precisely for this reason that much more can be learned from the earlier book, *Ahnung und Gegenwart* which, for all its faults, is an exuberant work into which the youthful author poured the effervescence of his sparkling mind and from which one can learn a great deal about his techniques, his ideology, and his general attitudes. This is particularly true since Eichendorff is one of those authors who, rather than developing or basically altering their artistic conception, prefer to distill and refine their fermenting poetic substance into ever greater achievements of craftsmanship. Compared with the earlier novel, *Dichter und ihre Gesellen,* for all its color and delightful mischief, is merely a more orderly reprise of old narrative techniques, motifs, themes, characters, and plots.

Ahnung und Gegenwart, conceived in 1811 and published in 1815, is by no means Eichendorff's greatest artistic accomplishment. But it is the great novel of his youth which contains the fullest statement of his concerns and in which one can find the seeds of almost all his later works. It is worth a thorough inquiry because here, the author's poetic devices, not yet manipulated with the synthetic skill of future years, are most easily recognizable.

The title is as appropriate as it is untranslatable into English. The term "Gegenwart" of course offers no problem. It refers to Eichendorff's own historical period with which he felt profoundly at odds. It is the present of the Napoleonic wars, the period of

rising national ambitions in Germany and of national humili-
ations as well—a present marked by the demise of the feudal
order and tinged with the ideas of the French Revolution, most of
which Eichendorff rejected. This German present, furthermore,
was dominated intellectually by a victorious Romanticism turned
shallow. The tenets of the Romantic creed, which Eichendorff
held sacred, were proclaimed, by a generation he regarded as
degenerate, from the fashionable salons of the residential capitals
he despised. That these same effeminate city dwellers should
raise the Christian flag did not endear them to Eichendorff in the
least, since he accused them of having lost the unshakable Christian faith of former, more substantial times, and of toying instead
with religious symbols in a noncommittal game.

So much for "Gegenwart," the definition of which is rendered
difficult only by a surfeit of concrete detail. It is the term "Ahnung" that presents the more serious obstacles. The dictionary
offers the translations "presentiment," "foreboding," and "hunch."
What it suggests in the context of the novel are the visionary elements, the intuitions about the past and the future of civilization
as Eichendorff saw them. They refer to history and poetry, politics, and salvation. The term "Ahnung" alludes to the fact that
Eichendorff saw in everything on earth a cipher for ultimate
religious truth. The present, for all its concreteness, seemed
more unreal to him than the past and the future, in the sense
that it was more distant from God than the two poles of the beginning and the end. Eichendorff visualized the trajectory of
human history as bending away from the divine; and only the
conviction that it emanated from God instilled in him the hope
that it would return to him. Thus, for him all action on the
secular stage was characterized by a fall from grace. This is
what he wanted to demonstrate in *Ahnung und Gegenwart* and
what the title of the novel so aptly suggests.

The first thing to be said about *Ahnung und Gegenwart* is that
it differs markedly from the realistic novels of the nineteenth
century and their successors in the twentieth, to which most
modern readers are accustomed. There is no firmly delineated
action, the characters are psychologically undeveloped, and
though the author attempts—as will presently be shown—to create
some sort of suspense, it is not of the kind generally encountered
in present-day fiction.

And yet there is much in this book to reward the persevering reader. Eichendorff was twenty-three years old when he conceived and twenty-four when he finished his work (twenty-seven when it appeared in 1815). Youthful playfulness and youthful seriousness enter into an unlikely but attractive alliance. Above all, the art of creating space and time and then linking them up by means of allegorical and symbolic devices, lends the work an unexpected density. Scenic and atmospheric values are handled appealingly, rich images abound, and the text is interspersed with many magnificent poems. Thus a great deal of poetic substance is manifest on almost every page, so that a particular secondary fascination is likely to captivate the reader who has successfully withstood the initial onslaught of boredom. Perhaps the best explanation of the book's nature and a possible motto for Eichendorff's art as a novelist is contained in the pages of *Ahnung und Gegenwart* themselves. Describing a period of extensive reading in his hero's life, the author has this to say in defense of the literary products with which he occupies himself:

Those are the best readers whose creative imagination keeps working with and beyond the book. For no poet offers a ready-made heaven; he merely sets up a heavenly ladder on this beautiful earth. Those too lazy and indolent to muster the courage of climbing upward on its light golden rungs will be precluded forever from bringing to life the mysterious letters, and would do better digging and plowing than idling their time away with useless reading.[1]

Whether or not Eichendorff consciously intended them to be an apology, these sentences, with all their moralizing and exalted metaphors, are applicable to the author's own efforts as a novelist. But, even more so, they describe quite accurately the frame of mind in which the reader ought to approach them.

I *Plot and Structure*

In the ordinary sense, *Ahnung und Gegenwart* does not have much of an action. The main characters are always on the move, but hardly do anything that would reveal personality or narrative purpose. If anyone had the superhuman memory to recall it all, the plot could at best be told in terms of where someone was *going*. As a matter of fact, the amount of movement is prodigious.

Every means of traveling known in the early nineteenth century is made use of, and I suspect that some of the methods were outmoded even then. It is difficult to think that quite so much walking and climbing up and down trees or mountains was going on in Germany, or anywhere in Europe for that matter.[2]

His characters are constantly in motion, either on horseback, in carriages, boats, or, of course, on foot. One night they will spend in a humble village inn, the next in an elaborate castle, the third in a haystack, and a fourth in a remote mill which is really a hiding-place for robbers. Their activities, so far as they cannot simply be subsumed under the heading of *Wanderschaft,* consist of hunting, singing, writing poetry, attending parties, and engaging in lengthy conversations.

Let us see what this does to the plot by attempting to narrate the action of the first few pages: Count Friedrich, accompanied by a few fellow students, is traveling down the Danube when they are overtaken by another ship with a beautiful and somewhat mysterious woman standing at the prow. At nightfall, the friends stop at an inn where the students set up camp in a rather disorderly fashion. To escape the noise and smoke Friedrich steps out on the balcony, where he finds himself side by side in the dark with the beautiful stranger from the other boat. He has just time to kiss her and find out that her name is Rosa, then they are separated.

The next morning, the students take leave of their companion, and Friedrich continues his journeys on horseback. At noon he reaches a well-kept public park situated on a hill. Just as he engraves Rosa's name on the window pane of a pavilion, he sees her at a great distance riding along a road toward the mountains. Although he follows her immediately, he loses track of her, and finds himself in an interminable forest. He takes a nap, from which he awakes at night. He continues until he reaches a forest inn. When he sees through a window that the main room is occupied by a crowd of disreputable-looking fellows, he does not enter but continues his nocturnal journey, which finally leads him to a mill. He is shown to a room by a pretty but—to Friedrich's Puritan tastes—all too scantily dressed girl who seems to have something on her mind. But he misinterprets her intentions, and she leaves without saying anything. His suspicions aroused, Friedrich lays his weapons in readiness and refrains

from going to sleep. Sure enough, soon his room is invaded by
the hoodlums he had observed earlier. In the ensuing fight, Friedrich is wounded. The last thing he sees before losing consciousness is the pretty girl defending him against the robbers with
a sword.

Subsequently, Friedrich awakens in a sumptuous castle, with
a handsome boy by the name of Erwin in his attendance. The
boy tells him that he had found him unconscious in the forest
the day before. A lady driving by in a coach had taken both of
them along after her servants had bandaged Friedrich. Questioned about his identity, the boy merely replies that he has no
parents, whereupon Friedrich hires him as his servant and companion. After this has been arranged, Friedrich arises and in-
spects the Old-Franconian castle and its garden with many
exotic flowers. He meets a stranger sitting and writing at a table
covered with papers, but is rudely turned away by him. In an
adjoining grove, he comes upon an attractive fifteen-year-old girl,
who sits on a dead deer and with a young hunter sings a duet
about hunting and loving. In their song, the hunting of a stag is
compared to the pursuit of a girl by her lover. They are hardly
finished when a whole hunting party, complete with dogs and
French horns, enters the scene, preceded by a handsome young
man, who turns out to be Leontin, the owner of the castle. Leontin informs Friedrich that it was his sister who brought him here
and, after spending a night at his bedside, she continued to her
own castle. He invites Friedrich to stay as long as he pleases. As
Friedrich is thanking his host, they are interrupted by background noises. Sheets of paper whirling through the air are followed by the man Friedrich had met writing in the garden.
Leontin shoots down some of the papers with his shotgun; but
before their owner is able to protest the destruction of his writings, he is distracted by the giggles of the pretty fifteen-year-old,
whom he tries to kiss but who escapes into the forest. Thereupon
the new arrival is introduced to Friedrich as the poet Faber with
whose work and reputation he is familiar. Now he finds it hard
to reconcile the slightly ridiculous figure with the great poet
whom he had always admired.

Leontin offers to take Friedrich to his sister, and Friedrich,
having recovered from his injury, accepts. On the way, Leontin
warns his new friend that his sister is old and ugly. Friedrich

is visibly disappointed, for in his feverish dreams he envisaged a lady with the features of an angel. He continues reluctantly. Soon they reach the lady's castle, a modern structure with a garden in the newest taste. Leontin sings a serenade to his sister. Friedrich, at first uninterested in meeting the old hag, hears a lovely voice responding from a window. He looks up and sees to his surprise—Rosa. While Leontin discreetly rides off on his sister's new horse, Friedrich accompanies Rosa, a dazzling beauty in negligée, to the garden, where they first exchange words, but soon proceed to increasingly ardent kisses. Leontin and Friedrich then ride back to the former's castle. They arrive in time to rescue Faber from a ludicrous dispute with one of the hunters over a French horn. In the evening, the three engage in a conversation about poetry in the course of which, true to his name, Faber propounds a poetics based on craftsmanship, whereas Leontin and Friedrich defend a theory of more spontaneous artistic creation. They are interrupted by Marie, the fifteen-year-old girl, who has disguised herself as a hunter's boy and is pursued by the other young hunters. Much to Friedrich's moral indignation, the scene climaxes in kisses and frivolous words being exchanged between Marie and Leontin. Before retiring for the night, Friedrich strums Leontin's guitar and sings a song out of his bedroom window.

This recapitulation covers the first three chapters, or twenty-five pages, of the novel, far less than one tenth of its total length. There is surely no point in continuing; but it should be obvious that one could go on and on without altering the tone or the method of narration. This kind of plot or nonplot is in every respect characteristic of *Ahnung und Gegenwart;* but of course not only of *Ahnung und Gegenwart.* Rather, Eichendorff adopted it from the Romantic novel which, by this time, was no longer new in Germany but had been well established and imitated since its introduction by Ludwig Tieck almost two decades earlier. (Many of its features were already present in Goethe's *Wilhelm Meisters Lehrjahre* of 1795 and 1796.) It would be grossly unfair to say that this absurd outline constitutes the substance of the novel. Its substance lies rather in exactly those elements which a recapitulation cannot capture: the landscape, the dreams, the dialogues and monologues, the allegorical passages, and, above all, the poems which continually interrupt the narra-

tive. But these are not parts of the plot, and the kind of plot
Eichendorff uses, has, I believe, been fairly represented.

Yet there is even more to the novel than this. Eichendorff
succeeded in imposing order and continuity upon this seeming
chaos by two means: subdivision and suspense. The term subdivision refers to the chapters and the three main parts or sections,
called "books." The chapters are generally very short—there are
twenty-four in a novel of less than three hundred pages—and
skillfully modeled. Usually a new chapter starts with a change
of scenery or a shift in perspective. It is either devoted to a new
character or written in a different key. The chapter endings are
also incisive: sometimes they coincide with the termination of a
day, at other times they are punctuated by a lyrical poem or a
carefully composed cadence. All this assists in varying and struc-
turing the monotony of the comings and goings provided by
the plot.

The three "books" into which the whole is divided have another but no less important function. Without strictly adhering
to such organization, they nevertheless present a three-phased
movement which does a great deal to enhance the intellectual
and artistic dignity of the novel. It might be possible to designate
the three steps corresponding to the three books as the personal,
the social, and the philosophical, each of which constitutes a
significant dimension of the entire work. Furthermore, each book
performs a function in the unfolding of the narrative which we
may call exposition, complication, and solution (or introduction,
expansion, and explication). In this manner, each book, though
based on its predecessor, represents a step into a higher conceptual sphere and is, at the same time, accompanied by a widen-
ing of the narrative horizon. That the three phases also correspond to Eichendorff's three theological categories, origin, alienation, and return, is their principal artistic merit. This is no mean
achievement for an incipient prose writer and goes a long way
toward counteracting the lack of a firm line of action.

It is worth delving a little more deeply into this question. The
first book introduces the main characters: Friedrich, Leontin,
Rosa, Faber, Erwin, Marie, Viktor, Julie and her family. But they
are all treated as individuals. Whenever the individual is transcended and relationships are delineated, it is always a question
of the relationship between two characters. This is a book of the

most uninhibited and unmotivated traveling. Toward its end, however, the action converges at the country estate of Herr von A. Here the reader gets a glimpse of the landed gentry, their family life, pleasures, worries, and ideals. This is an appropriate preparation for the next book, which mainly deals with problems of society. The predominant themes of discussion in the first book show a similar progression from the individual to the social. At first the conversations almost exclusively center around poetry and the creative process, but gradually they are replaced by subjects dealing with training and education.

The second book is set almost completely in the capital or "Residenz." While the plot suffers relapses into the earlier traveling, the number of excursions away from town is radically reduced, and it can be demonstrated that most of these are closely tied to the central theme of the book, the critique of the times. For example, Friedrich's visit to the castle of Countess Romana is the culmination of one of the primordial concerns of the novel, the effect of the prevailing erotic materialism on human life. But the point of the second book is that it is set in the city. Here lies its principal contrast to the first, which takes place entirely in the country. Needless to say, Eichendorff sees in country life the foundation of a healthy morality. In the tradition of Antonio de Guevara's *Libro de Menosprecio dela corte y alabança dela aldea (Book of Scorn for the Court and Praise for the Country,* 1539), and indeed of the classical authors of pastorals and idylls, the city and the court are for him repositories of evil and corruption. Therefore, the second could also be called the satirical book. Sexual mores, politics, the corrupt nobility, affected literature, and the literary *salons* come in for severe and sometimes amusing criticism.

It must be said at the outset that this criticism is much too vague and devoid of precise observation to be entirely successful, but there is no doubt that it represents Eichendorff's settling of accounts with his times which he accuses of being superficial, mendacious, lacking in courage, and oblivious of true religion. From the point of view of structure, this book constitutes an expansion of the first. A few new characters are introduced (the Prince, the Minister, the literary crowd and, most importantly, the allegorical figure of Romana is fully developed). The major characters of the first book, Leontin and Faber, are carried over but play a marginal role. However, the relationship of Friedrich and Rosa, the main love interest of the novel, is moved into the center and resolved. But here, too, the crucial aspect consists of the supra-individual factors working upon and destroying this love affair between two people seemingly predestined for each other. What separates them is precisely what constitutes the main issue of *Ahnung und Gegenwart,* the conflict between the old and the new.

Technically speaking, the third book brings the denouement, the fulfillment of all individual destinies; philosophically speaking, it offers the solution of all the riddles and the answer to all the problems that have been raised. The third book can thus be said to be one extended *anagnorisis.* Characteristically, the dialogue, as far as it is not intended to clear up the obscure past, revolves around life and religion. The conclusion is dedicated to the question of how the gifted individual should respond to his degenerate times. Eichendorff's answer is devastating: Friedrich turns his back on the community by becoming a monk, and Leontin by emigrating to America. It should be clear to the reader that in this context America is not a part of Western civilization but a kind of Rousseauistic Utopia, an image of the primitive, unspoiled good life.

From this analysis it ought to be clear that Eichendorff has succeeded in imprinting, by the skillful use of subdivisions, a powerful rhythm on his novel and in bringing it to an impressive climax.

Eichendorff's other ordering device is the technique of suspense. With its aid he attempts to energize a plot which is more lyrical than dramatic. By constantly hinting at mysteries, by gradually revealing hidden elements in the backgrounds of his characters, by setting up riddles which are solved only piecemeal, and by staging recognitions between separated friends and lost relatives, he tries to tie together distant parts of his story, thus showing an awareness that novels require a denser fabric than a plot mainly based on *wanderlust* can provide. But since the characters are insufficiently developed (or rather, since the function of character is not primarily psychological), all the reader experiences is the *desire* to create suspense, not the suspense itself.

An example seems to be in order. Early in the novel, a suspi-

cion is aroused that the boy Erwin is a girl in disguise and that
his abnegated devotion to Friedrich is love transmuted into sub-
servience. Throughout the book, this idea is nourished by reports
of Erwin's strange behavior which would be comprehensible
only if recognized as female jealousy. It is not until the third
book that Erwin is identified as the miller's girl, who so bravely
assisted Friedrich against the murderous robbers. And only at
the very end of the novel is it revealed that she also happens to
be Friedrich's niece, the daughter of his brother Rudolf and the
girl Angelina who played such an important role in Friedrich's
childhood. The suggestion of incestuous love, which this revelation contains, has been, through the ages, a literary cipher to
illustrate the insurrection of the senses and the unconscious
against morality which, in turn, explains the necessity to have
Erwin or Erwine end in insanity and premature death. In this
sense, the Erwin complex is tied up with one of the central concerns of *Ahnung und Gegenwart*. But since Erwine is never
brought to life as a believable character, since her existence is,
as it were, merely asserted and not proven, it remains a mere
strand of color in the kaleidoscope of the novel and therefore, no
matter how mysterious, fails to stir more than the mildest curi-
osity in the reader.

And so it is with everything. The entire fabric of the book is
interwoven with mysteries and enigmas. Friedrich's interest is
awakened by the beautiful stranger on the other boat. The same
evening, he kisses a pretty girl in the dark and learns that her
name is Rosa. She turns out to be the lady from the ship. The
next day he sees her from the top of a hill riding far away in
the distance. He follows and loses her. The day after he has been
wounded he is found unconscious in the forest by a lady driving
past in a carriage. Later he finds out it was Rosa. Friedrich finds
refuge in Leontin's castle who offers to take his new friend to
meet his rescuer, Leontin's "old and ugly" sister. She turns out
to be a dazzling beauty: Rosa. Their tempestuous but ill-fated
love affair extends throughout the novel. At the end, a final revelation is made. Before entering his monastery forever, Friedrich
sees a heavily veiled woman. The reader is informed that she is
Rosa, now the Crown Prince's wife. But Friedrich never finds
out. He is no longer interested in the affairs of this world. This
is, of course, a fine touch, but instead of being fascinated by the

deliberate designs of destiny—as Eichendorff's intention may have been—the reader is merely puzzled by the hidden meanings behind a surfeit of improbabilities.

Many of the characters harbor secrets. Leontin hides a secret in the forest, and not until the third book do we learn that it was a love affair and what effect it had on his life. Erwine's secret is compounded by a sub-secret: a male voice and a human shadow are perceived in her immediate vicinity by Friedrich; two hundred pages later we are enlightened. The nocturnal visitor was Rudolf, Erwine's father, but neither of the two had the slightest knowledge of their relationship. On every page, something unexpected, secretive, or amazing is related. A masked figure reminds the protagonist of someone he has known a long time ago; a voice has a familiar ring; somebody is sure to have seen a certain face before; or something is said with "striking vehemence." In the course of his confused meanderings through war-torn Germany, Friedrich comes to a castle where mad festivities are celebrated in spite of the destruction all around. The castle "happens" to be Romana's, and Friedrich shudders at this "coincidence."

Portraits mysteriously pointing to the most intimate occurrences in the lives of the central characters are favorite objects for the author. One day, in a perfectly strange castle, Friedrich sees an old painting of St. Anne teaching little Mary how to read. He is intrigued by it, "for the longer he looked at the quiet little head the more clearly all its features seemed to merge with those of a wellknown face. But this memory dated back to his earliest childhood, and he was unable to recall it exactly, much as he tried."[3] His inquiries are unfruitful and only when he finds his boy Erwin in girl's clothes does the mystery begin to lift: he recognizes Erwin's identity with the girl in the mill and, at the same time, realizes her striking resemblance to his childhood playmate Angelina. And Angelina—one finds out later—sat model for the little Mary in the picture which Friedrich had seen.

These few examples must suffice in the present context. They could be augmented almost at will. Of course, it would be naive to assume that their sole purpose is to create suspense, or that they are simply there because the model of the romantic novel after which *Ahnung und Gegenwart* is patterned requires this kind of mystification. They may be failures as exciting secrets which the reader is burning to see solved. But they are eminently successful in giving the impression that human existence is incomplete and confused if lived without a clear religious consciousness, and that a deeper truth lurks behind the surface appearances. It is precisely this tormented quest for clarification of the enigma that impels the main figures toward their self-fulfillment; and the great revelations at the end which meticulously bind together the fragments of the novel are perfect objective correlatives for the philosophical clarification and decision making that is taking place simultaneously. More will have to be said about this phenomenon which is so important to Eichendorff's art.[4] Suffice it at the moment to assert that his achievement as a writer consists in fusing an element of tradition (Romantic mystification) with an element of narrative technique (suspense), and in giving to both the symbolic force of representing his feeling of life.

II *Characters*

Sociologically speaking, the characters of *Ahnung und Gegenwart* belong, with very few exceptions, to the aristocracy. They include counts and countesses, country squires and their relatives, city people who obviously are members of the nobility, and an occasional prince. One principal character seemingly belonging to the lower classes, the miller's girl disguised as the boy Erwin, turns out to be Friedrich's niece and thus excellently pedigreed. Of course, the book is populated with students, traveling actors, hunters, peasants, soldiers, and servants but few of them rise above the category which the film industry staffs with "extras." Anyway, the action—insofar as the time is not spent floating down rivers or horseback riding through the countryside, which is another aristocratic pastime—takes place at the castles or in the town houses of the nobility. It need not be emphasized that none of the protagonists does a stroke of work as long as the novel lasts. Like those of medieval lords, their occupations are restricted to hunting, warring, traveling, and love-making.

One other activity must be mentioned: in the world of Joseph von Eichendorff, anyone worth his salt must be a poet. Of course, this is also a noble occupation and quite compatible with the medieval troubadour culture which the author so highly esteemed. But the principal figures—with the exception of Faber, whose character will require special attention—are certainly not professional writers: most of them aristocratically disdain to fix their poems in writing. They are well-born minstrels whose guitar playing and serenading is an idle and noble expression of their free souls. Obviously, this focus on the aristocracy is biographically motivated. Eichendorff was profoundly aware of the French Revolution, but its consequences interested him only insofar as they affected his own social class. While *Ahnung und Gegenwart* has many overtones of the political period novel, the historical moment is analyzed mainly as to its meaning for the nobility and, particularly, for its best representatives.

To say that Eichendorff's characters are partly male and partly female is neither a facetious nor a banally obvious statement, for men and women in this novel are given, perhaps unconsciously to the author, very different treatment. If one regards *Ahnung und Gegenwart* as a novel of salvation, a search for the right and just life—and it is imperative to regard it thus—one perceives that most of the male characters achieve an honorable way out of their own predicaments and those of their times, while the author does not tire of inventing ever new forms of degradation, shipwreck, and tragic death for his feminine characters. Erwine, the miller's girl, first turns mad and then dies of convulsive heart cramps. The Countess Romana, the most flamboyant and gifted female of them all, commits suicide after a dissolute life and vain attempts to expiate for her sinful inclinations in Christian repentance. Marie, the promising forest beauty, is finally passed from hand to hand as little more than a common tart. Rosa, Friedrich's erstwhile love, gives in to her baser nature, achieving worldly success by becoming the despicable prince's consort, but condemning her nobler self to perdition. The only exception is Julie, who is allowed to share her husband Leontin's heroic American exile, unimpaired in mind and body, but not before she has pledged, in a poetic but nonetheless serious vow, to remain, even in those remote parts, a faithful, self-sacrificing Teutonic maiden. She sings her romance "Of the German Virgin" in response to a question by Leontin which would be utterly tactless from a newly-wed husband if it were not so characteristic of Eichendorff's suspicious attitude toward women: "Will you be wholly a woman and, as Shakespeare says, submit to the unbridled drives that seize and tear you this way and that, or will you always have enough courage to subordinate your life to a higher ideal?"[5]

The men, on the other hand, fare much better. Unwilling to compromise with their degenerate contemporaries, Friedrich and Leontin achieve dignity by haughtily withdrawing from the scene, while Faber remains unperturbed and keeps on doing exactly what he has always done. The only shipwrecked male character is Robert. After fulfilling his function as chief explicator of mysteries, he rejects Friedrich's exhortation to seek his solace in religion. It must be presumed that he remains forever disgruntled. Whether marrying Rosa is meant as a punishment for the prince's many sins and hypocrisies must be left for the individual reader to decide. But whatever his verdict, he will agree that none of the heroes is as badly off as most of the heroines. The reason for this blatant inequality is simple enough. Its origin is the Christian, romantic-medieval mythology, from which Eichendorff derives his values. In this system, women are held to be closer to original sin than men. They are basically sensual creatures who have difficulty controlling their evil drives and consequently end in the abyss. They are beautiful but treacherous beings from whom sweet temptations emanate. But unless one makes a lucky find—that is the lesson to be learned from this novel—it is safer to stay away from them. This simple truth is driven home directly as well as symbolically. The fairy tale which Faber tells of Ida, the daughter of a pious knight who throws herself into worldly pleasure and ends as the wife of a ghastly water spirit, destroyed by the element, is such a symbolic reflection on women. Her destiny parallels, *mutatis mutandis*, that of many other female characters. The beautiful but uncanny Romana, whom Eichendorff allegorizes into a Venus figure, is another example, although her element is fire rather than water. This is also appropriate since the destructive force of Eros burns through the entire work, and it would not be implausible at all to approach *Ahnung und Gegenwart* from the point of view of its erotic symbolism.

What are Eichendorff's characters? Compared to the flesh-and-bone variety populating realistic fiction, they remain a shadowy lot. Each appears in a typical situation and is given a name, which is enough for his identification. Let us take Marie, the young forester's girl, as an example. She is first perceived through

Friedrich's eyes, sitting on a dead deer and singing a duet with a young hunter in which hunting is likened to the love play between the sexes, the quarry being identified as the female part. Marie and her situation form a picture which may be called an erotic emblem or pattern. From now on, whenever she appears, she is engaged in some sort of erotic activity, expecting or chased by a man, eluding a pursuer, mistaking one masked lover for another, defending the body of a dead lover, sometimes in tears and close to the recognition of her tragic plight, but mostly in gay, lighthearted abandonment to her function. This is precisely what she is: a function in a larger scheme with hardly a personality of her own.

The same can be said of a great number of minor characters in the novel. For example, Julie, Leontin's future wife, is assigned the role of the good female. If she escapes the fate of her many sisters, it is not because of any greater strength of character but due to her status as an unspoiled country baroness. The educational discussions revolving around her are not only intended to give vent to Eichendorff's views on the subject, but also to show how well Julie is equipped for the good life even though she has not benefited from the mundane education of the day. The only mystery allowed Julie is her being in love without the reader's knowing with whom. This facet, too, however, is calculated to reinforce her function in the total design: that of the "inner-directed" girl—if this expression is permissible—in her natural state, who is uncontaminated by the rotten "other-directed" culture and has the best chance to withstand the pernicious pressures of her sex.

What has been said about the minor characters holds largely true for the central figures as well. The difference is one of degree, not substance. Let us concentrate on Friedrich and Leontin, leaving Faber to the discussion of poetry, Romana to that of allegory. Rosa's part is so simple that it is difficult to think of her as a major figure, in spite of the large role she plays in Friedrich's life and consequently in the design of the novel. She is beautiful and can be tender like Julie. But her being is torn apart by a second tendency: social ambition and fascination with the superficial glamor of the court. That she allows Romana to lure her from Friedrich's company to the Residence is symbolic not only of the split in her personality but also of the direction

of her development. All the author has to do from that moment
on is to let her succumb more and more to her baser desires, to
the point of actually destroying her soul. All this is prefigured in
Faber's fairy tale of Ida, told in her presence and ostensibly as
a warning to her. Friedrich "could not refrain during the entire
story from thinking of Rosa with a vaguely pained feeling, and
it was his impression that Faber had chosen this tale with secret
intention."[6]

Essentially, the characters of Friedrich and Leontin are conceived in the same manner. They occupy more space in the novel.
Much of the story is told through them and for them; they also in-
tervene in considerably more situations and therefore seem more
complex. But, in fact, a very similar technique has been used in
their creation. All of this is connected with the nature of Eichendorff's plot as it has been described. Since the action does not
flow from the will power of the individuals but is a stereotyped
pattern superimposed upon them from without for the benefit of
a greater plan, the characters cannot possibly exhibit that three-
dimensional quality which we associate with spontaneous, self-
sufficient life. It is quite evident that Eichendorff did not employ
any of the many methods with which such an effect is achieved.
There is no analysis of emotions or thoughts, there are hardly
any inner conflicts and none of the little inconsistencies and subtle
contradictions that make a fictional construct spring to life. In
short, there is not a trace of psychology. Also lacking are the
various devices for expressing, mirroring, and faceting the personality in the exterior world which are so eagerly adopted by
writers more intent upon character creation than Eichendorff—
devices that show a figure as the author sees him, as he sees
himself, as he is seen by fellow characters, or as he expresses
himself in actions, conversation, dreams, diaries, and letters, in
sudden crises, and especially in conflict with other figures or the
world. Of this vast arsenal of techniques Eichendorff makes very
modest use. We learn about the main characters only the pre-
ciously few things which the author tells us in his own voice or
in their conversations, where a personalized tone is rarely attempted. One means of self-expression is, of course, the numerous poems and *Lieder* that are attributed to practically every
character in great abundance. It is a well-known and revealing
fact that many of these poems are lyrical masterpieces which

lead an independent existence in German literary history. Some
of their admirers are unaware or oblivious of the context in
which they originally appeared. But while these poems are
largely adapted, in thought and mood, to the occasions out of
which they arise, they are but an uncertain guide to an understanding of character.

The portrait of Count Friedrich, pieced together from its novelistic components, is not too difficult to reproduce. He first
appears in the company of his fellow students, and his creator
bestows heroic stature on him by asserting that "he was taller
than the others and distinguished by a simple and free appearance which was almost that of a medieval knight. He himself
spoke little, preferring to enjoy the frolics of his gay companions
quietly."[7] This is the principal description we have of him. He
is earnest, chaste, and restrained, and his author is so intent upon
making him a paragon of well-behaved morality that he sometimes dangerously resembles a Victorian spinster. This is particularly true in matters of sex, and the many thin night-gowns,
disarranged scarves, and semi-bare breasts of the novel throw
him into tizzies of moral indignation. When Leontin banters
with Marie, obviously to the girl's delight, we are told that "the
whole loose game pained Friedrich" and that "he loudly said
something about seduction."[8] But Friedrich's tendency to ser-
monize is not exclusively manifested in erotic circumstances. On
one occasion, while there is dancing and feasting on the second
floor of a country house, our two protagonists are outside, excluded from the festivities. Fortunately, a tall thick-leaved tree
opposite the windows offers a solution. "The tree is a veritable
Jacob's ladder," says the enterprising Leontin and climbs up.
But Friedrich disagrees. "Eavesdropping," he said, "especially
on joyful people in their pleasure, is always a bad and insidious
thing."[9]

It does not require much more than the above quotation to
show that Leontin is, in many respects, his friend's opposite.
While Friedrich is quiet, Leontin is boisterous; and where Friedrich is withdrawn, Leontin is meddlesome. One is passive, the
other active, one reflective and perseverant, the other enterprising, wild, impatient, and of a fiercely uncontrollable temperament. In fact, when Friedrich exhibits one character trait, Leontin
is endowed with its exact opposite, and this is also why he comes

closer to self-destruction than his friend. But basically, of course, the two have a great deal in common. They are both well-meaning, honest German barons, or rather resurrected medieval knights (one of them will become a monk, which is another favorite vocation of the Middle Ages), oriented towards the ideals of a bygone era who are suffering from the modern times, each according to his own temperament. Their final decisions are indicative of this mixture of sameness and divergence. On the surface, an active life in the new continent could not be more different from retreat into a monastery, but *au fond* both steps are identical in their indictment of the contemporary European scene. This reflection touches upon the secret of the two figures. They fit perfectly into the medieval model which has influenced much of Eichendorff's characterizations. Friedrich embodies the ideal of the *vita contemplativa,* Leontin that of the *vita activa.* In this respect they are opposites. But both ideals are different approaches to the one goal of Christian salvation, and in view of this shared purpose the divergence of their paths is by no means fundamental. This is why they appear static, without development, and allegorical.

Although many details have been left undiscussed, sufficient information has been given about Eichendorff's art of characterization. In this, as well as many other respects, he shows a tendency toward allegorizing. Each character seems to point beyond himself or herself to some abstract truth. Much speculation has gone into the attempt to associate the characters of *Ahnung und Gegenwart* with definite ideas. Is Rosa Romantic poetry or modern love? Does Romana represent paganism, unbridled phantasy, or is she a reincarnation of the Roman goddess Venus? For an understanding of the novel such unpoetic precision is not necessary. An insight into the principle is all that is needed. On the basis of the foregoing discussion it is now possible to reach the conclusion that Eichendorff's figures are not individual, psychologically developed, and motivated human beings with their contradictions and conflicts, nor are they intended to be such. They are, in fact, types endowed with a few fundamental traits that are more of metaphysical than of personal significance. They are ciphers or pawns in a great design: their author's scheme for salvation.

III *Symbolization*

It is quite obvious that ulterior meanings are attached to many of the poems which Eichendorff has inserted into his narrative; to some of the interpolated tales such as that of Ida, the bride of the water ghost; to certain localities, like Rudolf's castle at the end of the novel with its curious inhabitants who, just like their host, are torn between the ethos of ancient times and the moral dearth of their own; and even to the descriptions of certain landscapes and personalities. There has been discussion among Eichendorff scholars whether to call these tendencies symbolic or allegorical.[10]

The very beginning of *Ahnung und Gegenwart* offers an excellent example. The first sentence of the novel, which reports the rise of the sun and the progress of a ship down the Danube, is not likely to arouse suspicions. But near the end of the first paragraph, when the narrator dramatically abandons his role as a seemingly objective observer and adds his own undisguised commentary, one realizes that the mood of careless frivolity and youthful mischief is not there for its own sake alone but as a contrast to a more serious attitude toward life soon to be introduced. The words "Und so fahre denn, frische Jugend! Glaube es nicht, dass es einmal anders wird auf Erden" (Travel on, unspoiled youth! Never mind that things will change someday on earth)[11] establish an enormous distance between the author and this scene, reducing it to a vignette which he intends to manipulate in order to bring out some abstract truth.

After the individualized statements of the first paragraph, the generalizing opening of the second one strikes a well-calculated mood of solemn significance, and it is now that the allegory central to the entire novel is unfolded.

Wer von Regensburg her auf der Donau hinabgefahren ist, der kennt die herrliche Stelle, welche der Wirbel genannt wird. Hohe Bergschluften umgeben den wunderbaren Ort. In der Mitte des Stromes steht ein seltsam geformter Fels, von dem ein hohes Kreuz trost-und friedenreich in den Sturz und Streit der empörten Wogen hinabschaut. Kein Mensch ist hier zu sehen, kein Vogel singt, nur der Wald von den Bergen und der furchtbare Kreis, der alles Leben in seinen unergründlichen Schlund hinabzieht, rauschen hier seit Jahrhunderten gleichförmig fort. Der Mund des Wirbels öffnet sich von Zeit zu Zeit dunkelblickend, wie das Auge des Todes. Der Mensch fühlt sich auf einmal verlassen in der Gewalt des feindseligen, unbekannten Elements, und das Kreuz auf dem Felsen tritt hier in seiner heiligsten und grössten Bedeutung hervor.

Whoever has traveled down the Danube from Regensburg, knows the magnificent place called the Whirlpool. Steep forest ravines surround the wonderful site. In the middle of the river stands a strangely shaped rock from which a tall cross looks down, full of solace and peace, into the surge and strife of the mutinous waves. Not a person is to be seen here, not a bird is singing, only the forest covering the mountains and the dreadful circle which pulls all life down into its unfathomable gullet, have been rustling here monotonously for centuries. From time to time the mouth of the vortex opens up, gazing darkly, like the eye of death. All at once man feels lost in the power of the hostile, unknown element, and the cross on the cliff emerges in its greatest and most sacred significance.[12]

No one accustomed to read a novel on a level only slightly deeper than that of mere plot, will fail to understand the momentous meaning of this passage. But what exactly is it that forces the reader to see in this description of landscape a paradigm of man's alternatives in life? Why does the turmoil of the waters assume a human meaning and suggest a turbulent, directionless existence, the eddy that of a threat to peaceable progress, and the cross the promise of salvation? Superficially, of course, the entire scene remains within the frame established in the first paragraph: a journey down a river. Eddy, rock, and cross are elements of a landscape which a topographical investigation may well reveal to be a feature of the Danube below Regensburg. But a variety of signals contrives to extend the purport of the sentences beyond their surface meaning. For one thing, there is the abrupt change of key which precedes the allegorical passage and at the same time serves as a hint as significant things to come. The choice of adjectives is a further means to create contrast. The place is called "magnificent" in the introductory sentence and again, in apparent synonymy, "wonderful." Yet in German "wunderbar" also means miraculous, a connotation reinforced by the presence of the cross. When the author says that it "looks down full of solace and peace" into the river, he goes beyond the requirements of pure description. Certainly, solace and peace are traditional attributes of religious faith and inject a spiritual element into the scene. How calculated this effect is becomes especially apparent through the contrast with the attributes of the waves, which are said to be "empört," churned up, mutinous (with strong connotations of emotional turmoil and insurrection), and engaged in "Sturz und Streit"—"surge and strife," an expression whose contradictory composition of mechanical and emotional categories is smoothed over by the alliteration binding them together in mock harmony.

By proclaiming the peace and solace emanating from the cross, Eichendorff emphasizes its symbolic and non-natural character, lifting it, as it were, out of its immediate setting into a different sphere of the imagination. This logic and the skillful manipulation of attributes compels the reader to regard the waves, too, as only a symbol of some sort of higher reality, just as the cross stands for Christ and the Church. What element, contrasted with the solace and peace of religion, is found in such turmoil, he unwittingly asks; and the following details of description, carefully chosen for their emotional and connotative properties, gradually suggest an answer. The eddy is a "dreadful circle which pulls all life down into its unfathomable gullet." Is it Nature or Life that is embodied in this elemental phenomenon? Such, at least, are the abstractions that forcibly come to mind. The horror is accentuated by the sudden desolation of a scene which was teeming with life and gay with noises only a short while ago: "Not a person is to be seen here, not a bird is singing." Man's impotence in the face of a devouring threat (suggested by nouns such as "mouth" and "gullet") is further emphasized by the reference to lapses of time which vastly exceed the limited span of his life ("have been rustling here monotonously for centuries"). Thus one can add Time, which inexorably engulfs us, to the abstractions that have been hovering over the passage.

Another device employed by Eichendorff is that of comparison, likewise unsuited to a strictly realistic description of scenery, but very effective in creating the allegorical meaning. "From time to time," one reads, "the mouth of the vortex opens up, *gazing darkly*." At first, the reader accepts this peculiar gerund as a form of mood-creating synesthesia or Romantic mixing of the metaphors of sense perception, only to realize shortly that the "gazing darkly" also serves as a link with the comparison "like the eye of death" which, in turn, is an important piece in the entire black-and-white mosaic.

As if afraid that the symbolic significance of all this might be missed, Eichendorff now abandons, for a moment, the realm of objects in which he has pretended to be moving, and enters into the sphere of ideas, frankly interpreting his panorama: "All at once, man feels lost in the power of the hostile, unknown element, and the cross on the cliff emerges in its greatest and most sacred significance." He still has not said—and could not say without destroying the passage artistically—what the "unknown element" exactly is. But he has been utilizing an age-old system of metaphors which is well understood by all those who are even vaguely acquainted with the traditions of religious writing. Man's ship of existence is traversing the treacherous and often turbulent waters of life threatening to engulf the heedless voyager who is intent only upon the pursuit of his pleasures. If, however, he chooses to navigate by the cross of Christ, erected on the rock of the Church, he will avoid shipwreck and reach the harbor safely.[13] Eichendorff's merit as a narrator is to have woven the various threads of this allegorical tradition into the fabric of his own work, and to have endowed a boat trip on the Danube with the philosophical meaning characteristic of his entire novel. No wonder that the students, dimly aware of such hidden significance, give up their boisterous behavior and lapse into a reflective attitude: "Everybody became silent at this sight and breathed deeply over the roaring of the waves."

But there is more to come. If things were this simple, Friedrich's, the protagonist's, tormented odyssey through nearly another three hundred pages of *Ahnung und Gegenwart* would be unnecessary, since there would be no impediment to his entering the monastery immediately. But the allegory continues in order to introduce the counterforce, which is to delay, but of course not to prevent, his rapprochement with salvation. "Another strange ship" suddenly approaches Friedrich's vessel. Logically, the adjective "strange" is superfluous in the context, for the reader knows that it could not be the hero's own ship. But the connotations of "alien" and "uncanny" that the German word "fremd," as well as its English equivalent, carries are preparatory for the turn the allegory is taking. Remaining within the equa-

tion ship = life, the writer is telling his readers that a second
human existence, alien to his, is crossing the hero's path. There
can be no mistake about the significance of the woman standing erect at the ship's bow. Her eyes meet Friedrich's in a fateful
glance which conjures up for him a "miraculous world of luxuriant blossoms," awakening "old, old memories" (uralte Erinner-
ungen), and kindling in his heart "desires never known before."

The sinister force of these allurements is immediately asserted,
for the young woman fixedly stares into the eddy of turbulent
waters, thus revealing her affinity—perhaps identity—with the
destructive element. The unwary students are easily overcome
by the attraction of her appearance and break out in joyful, fra-
ternity-like cheers as she passes by. But Friedrich, allegorically
towering over his comrades, is also more sensitive and more vul-
nerable. He is struck in his innermost being by this encounter
with the beautiful stranger. The German verb "fuhr zusammen"
(more dynamic than the English "started") registers the sudden
impact. It is necessary to recall the blunt attributes Eichendorff
uses to characterize the figure at the prow: "tall, young, and
female." As the novel unfolds, one is made to face, again and
again, women whose being is equaled with the indomitable drive
of the senses. In this as well as other works by Eichendorff, the
demonic woman's kinship with the destructive element, be it
water or fire, is a recurrent motif. But like everything magical,
the enigmatic girl is ravishing as well as threatening. Her appearance kindles Friedrich's lust for life and makes him inattentive
to the change in the landscape from the highly dramatic gorge to
an innocuous and pacific scenery of beautiful castles and villages,
pastures and grazing herds: "He was sunken in her sight for a
long while and scarcely noticed that the river had meanwhile
turned calmer again and that on both sides beautiful castles,
villages, and meadows flew past, from where the wind blew over
the ringing of cowbells of grazing herds."

At this point, the reader does not learn who the beautiful
stranger is. Yet there comes a moment in the narrative when
Venus herself crosses the protagonist's path. But Venus is in
every woman, and we later learn that Rosa, who the sailing lady
turns out to be, is a "relative" of the Countess Romana, also a
femme fatale and the allegorical embodiment of the goddess
of love.

Here, at the beginning of the great novel of his youth, Eichendorff has clearly identified the danger of becoming involved, and finally lost, in the world with the erotic impulse, as something coming from or concentrated in women. Reversing Goethe's famous dictum in order to adapt it to Eichendorff, one might say: "Das Ewig-Weibliche zieht uns hinab!" (The Eternal-Feminine pulls us down!). The directional adverb "hinab" assumes almost literal force if we relate it to the eddy into which the woman at the prow stares and which also threatens to pull Friedrich under. The rest of the novel is a slow and colorful spinning out of this masterful allegory.[14] Of course, it is not the last one by any means. Allegorizing is one of Eichendorff's irrepressible habits as a writer, and this tendency is detectable in every aspect of his compositions. The public becomes "Mr. Public" for him, the Rococo is turned into a "Prince Rococo," Aurora is personified more than once and endowed with divine characteristics, while Europe is changed into the "Jungfrau Europa" which, in turn, makes it possible to make a "whore" out of her.[15] Mass scenes, individual characters, and even landscapes (as we have seen) are apt to sparkle allegorically under Eichendorff's hands.

A brief examination of some of the personal names used in *Ahnung und Gegenwart* will show that even they are tinged by this propensity of their inventor. The very absence of last names is significant. Neither Friedrich's nor Leontin's and Rosa's family names are revealed, and the abbreviation "von A." is used for the members of Julie's family. In the choice of family names, more than with Christian names, an author must commit himself to a more naturalistic or more symbolic practice. Friedrich, the central character's name, seems devoid of hidden meanings at first glance. But, reflecting on his personality, one is inclined to conclude that his widely accepted name, at home in all social classes of Germany and represented in all historical periods, including the Middle Ages, is most appropriate for its bearer's function in the novel. All his qualities, including his simple, unpretentious, Old-Franconian nature, are confirmed by it.

The opposite is true of Faber, the Latin word for craftsmanlike or artful. This name, not much in currency, points unerringly to his role as a professional poet with a decided orientation toward craftsmanship. Equally unmistakable is Romana's name with its suggestion of Italy and pagan mythology, but also of Roman-

ticism. Her role will be discussed at greater length further on in
this chapter. Here it is sufficient to stress that Italy, with its connotations of heathendom and eroticism—traditional in German
letters—epitomizes the forces antagonistic to Christianity in a
number of Eichendorff's works, and that the Countess combines
these elements admirably. Rosa's name does not demand any
etymological erudition either. Still, it is more skillfully chosen
than may be immediately apparent because the appealing Latin
word which constitutes it is somewhat counteracted by the fact
that it shares its first syllable with that of Rosa's "relative" Romana, thus subtly suggesting the ambivalent character of its
bearer. The Latin associations of Leontin's name also allude to
the properties of fierce independence and restless activity which
characterize the novel's second protagonist in general.

It is neither possible nor necessary to cover the entire field of
allegorical allusions in *Ahnung and Gegenwart*. Once the manner
has been understood, the reader will have no difficulty in making
the proper mental transpositions wherever called for. However,
because of their central importance as well as their complexity,
a rapid survey of the allegorical implications of the figure of the
Countess Romana must be made here. It will serve, at the same
time, as an example of Eichendorff's use of novelistic character
for allegorical purposes.

The first reference to Romana is already characteristic: she
lures Rosa from Friedrich's side and takes her to the court capital,
where she gradually succumbs to the temptations of superficial
amusements, sex, and social rank. Not surprisingly, it is in Book
Two, devoted to a critique of contemporary society, that Romana
is introduced as an active character. On the one hand, she is a
personification of the pagan goddess of love, and in addition to
her name there are other indications of her intended mythical
reincarnation of Venus. In a tableau—itself an allegorical representation of the great forces in conflict—she impersonates "a
beautiful female figure in Greek attire, as the ancients depicted
their goddesses. She was enveloped by colorful, rich flower gar-
lands and held up a cymbal with both arms raised as if for dancing, so that the entire symmetrical fullness and magnificence of
her limbs became visible. Having turned her frightened face
away from Glory (the representation of Christianity), she was
illuminated only in part; but still she was the most distinctive

and perfect of the figures. It seemed as if earthly, sensuous beauty, touched by the radiance of heavenly beauty, had thus suddenly frozen into her bacchantic attitude."[16] Image and commentary leave nothing to be desired in the way of clarity. That the Countess should be called "the beautiful heathen"[17] and compared to "an Italian improviser"[18] is further confirmation of her role. Her beauty is described as "lavishly rich" and "Southern," her movements as "fiery," her eyes as "large, burning, penetrating . . . and sweeping over Friedrich like a magnet."[19]

But there is more to her than this. In the longest poem of the book, consisting of 196 partly rhyming and partly assonant verses, which she recites at the literary soirée, Romana cryptically refers to other attributes of her own. According to its formal elements, the poem is an allegorical romance or ballad, an allegory in an allegory (it is specifically referred to as an allegory by one of the listeners[20]). Wild speculation as to the identity of the central personage in the poem, called a "princess" and a "sorceress" by Romana, follows the recitation. That she is intended to represent Romana herself would be evident even if Eichendorff did not say through Friedrich that "it is probably the Countess herself." But some of the other interpretations do not lack in validity either. "Is she not Poetry?" someone asks, and "Some took the princess to be Venus, others called her Beauty, others called her the Poetry of Life."[21] In part, the romance is an embroidery of the medieval legend in which the sorceress Venus lures young men to her mountain castle in order to destroy them. But the main point here is that Venus-Romana is not only a destructive, but also a life-giving, poetry-creating force, herself irresistibly attracted to Aurora, the mythical embodiment of the powers of origin and morning, an "eternal bride of Earth."[22] She realizes that her innocent relationship with nature has been tragically impaired by the advent of a false and feeble modern age. What was once poetic heroism (the allegorical heroes assembled at the Princess' court are historical and legendary knights, indiscriminately mixed, with Don Quixote, both a knight and a poetic fiction, as their prototype), has degenerated into pseudo-poetry. On the basis of her great poem, one can recognize in Romana an indomitable life force, a natural force of phantasy that is destined to come to a tragic end not only because of its paganism but also because of an anemic present which has no room for such vitality.

It corresponds to this composite character that Friedrich finds Romana "attractive and repulsive at the same time."[23] Far from being a mere representation of modern times and corrupt social and poetic practices, as some have thought, she is portrayed as towering over everyone in the mercilessly satirized milieu of the capital city. From certain passages one gains the inevitable impression that more than anyone else in the entire book Romana has a deep understanding of Friedrich's soul:

Friedrich stood among these blurred existences like a vigorous hunter in the fresh beauty of morning. Solely the Countess Romana attracted him. The very poem she had recited had made him attentive to her and the characteristic bent of her mind, which was so different from all the others. Even then he had thought to detect in it a deep contempt and an acute ability to see through the whole tea party, and his conversations with her now confirmed this opinion. He was amazed at the freedom of her views and the boldness with which she understood and treated all people. With incomprehensible liveliness she had instantaneously penetrated all the ideas Friedrich had touched upon in his earlier remarks, and she now met all his thoughts halfway. There was a magic wealth in her mind as well as in her beautiful body; nothing in the world seemed too big for her heart; she showed a deep, enthusiastic insight into life and all the arts, and for this reason Friedrich conversed with her exclusively for a long time, forgetting the others present.[24]

This is no common Venus and one senses her profound attraction not only for the central character but for the author himself. These brilliant attributes are, of course, very much a part of the temptation. Eichendorff does not spare any efforts to impart a feeling for its strength.

The whole relationship comes to a climax when Friedrich, responding to her repeated invitations, pays the Countess a visit at her castle. Already his approach is full of suggestive detail. Friedrich is first reminded of his childhood by the landscape (with Eichendorff invariably a sign of emotional involvement); then he is trapped in a deep gorge and realizes that "he must have taken the wrong path."[25] At this point, a whole episode, involving a group of actors, a former fellow student of Friedrich's, and his unfaithful sweetheart, is interposed, all of which serves to illustrate the destructive power of Eros. Finally, Friedrich reaches the castle and is struck by a scene replete with symbolism. The castle towers "like a work of witchcraft" high above an "indescribable chaos of gardens, vineyards, trees, and rivers . . . where countless water fountains sprang forth from the green." Obviously a vegetative world is conjured up, with the accent on the chaotic, uncontrolled impulses of nature. The motif of the vineyards is repeated and subsequently expanded to the point of acquiring the force of a bacchic symbol. The palace is built in the Baroque style with masses of marble and rows of columns. "Strange, foreign trees and plants" and "foreign birds" add an artificial flavor. They are compared to "half-expressed, bewitched thoughts."[26] That the sun should set upon this scene and a romantic night descend upon it, is calculated as part of the setting. (Eichendorff's atmospheric effects will be discussed in the next section.) Friedrich surveys this landscape and hears the "exulting cries of the vintagers." His reaction to the beauty and gaiety of the scene would strike one as incongruous if one had lost the total design of the episode from sight, for the reader is informed that Friedrich became unspeakably dejected at this sight.[27]

With the arrival of Romana-Venus, with a boy representing Cupid, the actual seduction begins. Baskets full of grapes, Italian terraces, fragrances, and a wealth of other detail combine to lull Friedrich's consciousness and excite his senses. He "felt like a sleepwalker, who suddenly wakes up from heavy, unbelievable dreams in an unfamiliar place."[28] "The sorcery of this evening affected . . . Friedrich's heart," and we are not amazed to learn that "in this sense-confusing intoxication he found the beautiful woman at his side seductive for the first time."[29] But the seduction does not take place. Friedrich's innocence protects him by arousing fears and revulsions. The Countess' physical proximity, her obvious desire, a mirror in Friedrich's bedroom in which he can see his hostess undress in a neighboring chamber—all this is to no avail and he simply goes to sleep.

But the supreme test is yet to come. In the middle of the night he wakes up and, to his surprise, hears breathing near him. "He looked around and saw Romana, undressed as she was, sleeping at the foot of his bed. She rested on the floor, leaning one arm and half her body against the bed. The long black hair flowed undone over her white neck and breasts." Understandably, Friedrich "observed the marvelous figure . . . full of wonderment."[30] This is the most critical moment, and Eichendorff does not tell us what would have happened if the sounds of a song had not reached Friedrich's ears. But the song does come. It always does. No matter how often Eichendorff repeats this situation,[31] it always ends in the same way: a poem of strongly Christian content is intoned, shattering the pagan magic and delivering the tantalized hero. The particular poem that frees Friedrich is sung by Leontin. Providentially, it does away with what is attracting him by means of the *vanitas-vanitatum* argument: "Where is the woman's beauty gone?" and rises to the Biblical: "Does no one want to wake with me?" The key stanza is the fourth since, in it, the idea of Christ is opposed to that of the world:

> Wie weit die falsche Welt auch sei,
> Bleibt mir doch einer nur getreu,
> Der mit mir weint, der mit mir wacht,
> Wenn ich nur recht an ihn gedacht.

> However wide the false world be,
> There is only one who is true to me,
> Who cries with me, who wakes with me,
> If I only think of him with intensity.

But the last stanza is also important because it establishes the theological significance of the morning:

> Frisch auf denn liebe Nachtigall,
> Du Wasserfall mit hellem Schall!
> Gott loben wollen wir vereint,
> Bis dass der lichte Morgen scheint!

> Up, up then, lovely nightingale,
> Up, waterfall with your bright sound!
> United shall we praise our God
> Until the radiant morning shines![32]

This is enough to bring Friedrich to his senses. The irresistible appeal of the song is understandable. It combines two major forces in Friedrich's life (which he himself cites in the story of his childhood,[33] paralleled in Eichendorff's own life): poetry and religion. Once and for all liberated he flees from Romana's house. Outside "he breathed deeply as he rode into the magnificent night, his soul felt as if freed from a thousand chains."[34]

A glance at Romana's further destiny will suffice. In love with Friedrich, cognizant of her failure to captivate him and aware of a terrible deficiency in her life, she tries to repent and turn to religion, but fails. "Venus Christianized" is an absurd thought. She then ends in total dissoluteness and suicide. Of utmost importance is the sentence by means of which Eichendorff conveys her desperate failure as she realizes that she cannot attain Friedrich's "virtue and greatness." "The two unruly horses hitched to her life," we read, "the black one and the white one, again bolted at this sight, carrying her along; all her beautiful intentions lay smashed under the hot wheels of her carriage, she let go of the reins and gave herself up"[35]

This is the allegorical method in quintessence. There are, of course, no such horses. They are introduced only for their power of signification. Their opposing colors are capable of suggesting the contradictory tendencies in Romana's mental makeup. Equally characteristic of the allegorical mode is the mixing of concrete detail with abstract notions. The horses "bolt" at the sight of "virtue and greatness," "intentions" are smashed under "hot wheels," the horses are "hitched" to Romana's "life."

To be successful, even such a fleeting allegorical image must satisfy two needs. There must be a philosophical point of comparison, a *tertium comparationis* as the older manuals would say, and a concrete connection with the context, something that one might call an "ecological link." Both conditions obtain here. The *tertium comparationis* is the same one which Eichendorff uses so frequently: life is a journey, a carriage is "the vehicle of life" (it is interesting to note how to a certain extent the allegory works by itself, forcing the writer into connecting abstract concepts with concrete images). The ecological factor can be seen in that a horse-drawn carriage is very much a part of Romana's style of living and the whole idea of swift recklessness perfectly attuned to her temperament. This prerequisite prevents the allegory from appearing "farfetched" or "stilted."

In *Ahnung und Gegenwart,* the Venus allegory is not fully developed.[36] In his later works Eichendorff will combine it most skillfully with the allegory of Italy, a syndrome which will be discussed at a later point in our investigation. In this early novel, the two realms are still essentially separate. The Romana episodes take place in Germany and must, therefore, remain content with a few allusions associating them with Rome and the South. Italy, on the other hand, with its enchanting but destructive effect on the Northern Christian, is conjured up at the end of the narrative in the story of Rudolf's life. Needless to say, it is a peculiar, highly stylized Italy with more meaning than empirical substance (Eichendorff never went there): in other words, another allegory.

Wherever the word "allegory" was used in the above analysis, another writer might have preferred the expression "symbol." All these terms have become ambiguous through imprecise and excessive use in the course of a long critical history. As a matter of fact "allegorical" is now used as a derogatory word by a great many German literary historians. The origin of its pejorative meaning is to be found in Goethe, who attributed creative properties to the "symbol," while discrediting "allegory" as a rationalistic and mechanical device of craftsmanship. It would be inappropriate to discuss the merits of his argument in detail. What symbol and allegory have in common is that they are both devices by means of which the author manages to impart to his words a meaning transcending their immediate context, thus giving a much broader significance to them. Whether one prefers to speak of symbolizing or allegorizing depends, in my opinion, on the degree to which such passages are integrated with the empirical elements used to build up a fictional world. Symbols are fused to the point of being indistinguishable from the qualities that are mimetic of the "real" world. The more realistic a work, the more symbolic it is, therefore, apt to be.

If I have preferred the term "allegory" for describing Eichendorff's procedure, I did so because of the relative arbitrariness and independence of the objects in that author's fictional world or, put differently, because of their doubtful "realism." Objects of sense perception become strangely transparent in Eichendorff's hands. The entire physical world in which man's terrestrial life is bound to take place, and which can be juicily robust and self-sufficient in other writers, becomes, in his workshop, a flimsy, diaphanous veil through which the great spiritual meanings shine powerfully at all times. These are often so pervasive that they rob the surface phenomena, delightful as they are, of much of their solid material impenetrability. The strength of these ideas derives from their connection with a theological system which was prevalent in the Middle Ages. Then, as in Eichendorff's poetic cosmos, the pagan and the Christian ways of life were engaged in a fierce struggle. The Body and the Soul, Earth and Paradise, the Here and the Hereafter fought their battles over man's allegiance. The mechanism which the medieval poets utilized in order to embody their abstract ideas were also allegorical. As soon as we give up the somewhat primitive notion that allegory is a woman entering the stage with a sash across her chest inscribed "Virtue," we shall be rid of an obstructive prejudice. Since Eichendorff endows the world he describes with only a very few, forever repeated features, since a country like Italy, which plays an important role in his poetic cosmos, is made up of an amazingly narrow field of sense data, and every woman in his repertory of characters can turn into Venus—the goddess herself, not a feeble, metaphorical Venus-like creature—I have decided to call Eichendorff's manner allegorical.

In an extended sense, it is possible to say that the entire novel, rather than being a representation of historical reality, is an allegory of life during the Napoleonic era. The focus on history derives from the point of view of the aristocracy, and while a great many values are posited, the verdict pronounced on the times is devastating: for the unspoiled individual belonging to that social class life has become intolerable. His hopes lie either in monastic seclusion or emigration. However, as far as the writer's success in communicating with his audience is concerned, we possess a number of testimonies.[37] The tributes paid to *Ahnung und Gegenwart* by Eichendorff's contemporaries show that for them, in a manner no longer comprehensible to us, the novel seems to have reflected with insuperable precision, not the historical details to be sure, but the true mood and climate of the period in which the action is set. This is, indirectly, also a tribute to the suggestiveness that can be achieved by means of an allegorical representation.

IV *Other Poetic Devices*

The little tricks of the trade, the consciously employed methods every author must resort to in order to tell his story, but also those subtler and probably unwitting poetic impulses which one might call the writer's style, constitute the poetic flesh of the work. The larger questions of structure, plot, and philosophy would correspond to the bone, if we remain in the same sphere of imagination. It is in the flesh that the phenomena of life appear to us, and it is on the flesh, with all its delights and deceptions, that we must exercise our perceptive qualities.

Much of what might seem to fall into this category is not Eichendorff's own possession or invention. No writer lives in a vacuum, and for most of them the world in which they move and from which they draw their raw materials includes a literary climate, i.e., one or several poetic traditions. This ingredient in Eichendorff's craft was supplied, in the main, by the Romantic school, with some of whose first and second generation practitioners and theoretical proponents he entered into significant relationships. The large outlines of Eichendorff's prose narratives are those of the German Romantic novel, of which, by the time he wrote his first work, the examples of Jean Paul Richter, Tieck, Novalis, and Brentano[38] to mention only the most outstanding ones, were available to him. Whether one calls Goethe's *Wilhelm Meister* a Romantic novel or not, is beside the point. It was *against* the content but *in* the form of *Wilhelm Meisters Lehrjahre* that the Romantics—without ever attaining a comparable degree of artistic mastery—wrote their novels of development and initiation. Thus Goethe's novel forms, at least in practice, an extremely important part of the Romantic tradition, and the two influences on a later writer are rather inseparable. Nevertheless, if one insists on singling out individual features, one can point to a particularly striking example, among many others, in the figure of Erwin in *Ahnung und Gegenwart*. The girl in boy's clothes who is in love with her master and whose mind is so overly delicate that it is first deranged and then leaves its body prematurely, whose past is too mysterious and whose hold on this earth too precarious for a well-balanced existence, would never have been created without the model of Goethe's Mignon from whom all of these traits are derived.

Another literary echo in *Ahnung und Gegenwart*, although of a much more peripheral nature, comes from Cervantes, whose great novel had, long before Eichendorff, achieved the status of gospel for the German Romantics. They adored the grotesque knight who is roaming the landscape with his incredible horse and who, in all his madness, possesses more wisdom than the sane philistines who dare make fun of him.

Apart from these details, Eichendorff's novel exhibits traits that one must call Romantic without need for singling out a specific model. The lack of character delineation and development, the avoidance of detailed realistic observation, the interminable journeys of the heroes in place of a firmly constructed plot—these are Romantic rather than specifically Eichendorffian weaknesses. And the interruption of the narrative flow by interpolated tales, autobiographical reminiscences, letters, dreams, and poems can be observed in any of the Romantic novels of the period.

Compared to this complexity of the genre, the actual act of story-telling is simple enough. In this respect, Eichendorff does not significantly deviate from the practice of his predecessors either. Most of his novel is told in the tone of straightforward reporting: a person does or says so and so. The thoughts of his characters are as intimately known to their author as are their overt actions. The perspective is fairly consistently that of the figure who happens to be in the center of attention. There is no difference in narrative technique between happenings told by the author in the third person and first-person reports placed in the mouths of individual characters, usually about their own past lives.

Poems are frequently introduced by phrases like: "Then she sang the following song" or "in the night he heard a masculine voice recite the following poem." This device is quite primitive when someone relates events in the distant past and not only remembers the exact moment when to recite the innumerable poems he has heard, but recalls verbatim their texts as well. In the case of poems sung by someone other than the reminiscing character, Eichendorff usually is aware of the patent improbability of total recall and often adds, in explanation, something to this effect: "I immediately recognized the song because I had taught it to her myself." At fairly frequent intervals, the author adds a phrase reminding his readers that it is he who is telling them a story, such as: "Let us now turn to," "We shall likewise turn to," "as we have seen," or "as we know." But sometimes he abandons the reportorial tone altogether and comments on the events in his own voice as a human being who brings to the story his own wisdom and his own emotions, as in the beginning, when he addresses the students: "Travel on, unspoiled youth! Never

mind that things will change someday on earth!" We have seen,
however, that even this seemingly spontaneous outburst is put
to good narrative effect.

The best passages in the novel are those where report and comment, empirical facts of observation and the author's critical attitude, melt in one coherent whole. This invariably occurs in mass
scenes such as weddings, masked balls, and social gatherings of
one sort or another, often with humorous or satirical effects.
Eichendorff is a master of these chaotic grotesqueries and is
undoubtedly in his very own element there, although models for
similar descriptions could be found in the works of Clemens
Brentano.

Entirely original, however, is Eichendorff's treatment of the
times of day, which is so elaborate and so central to his work
that it constitutes something akin to a private myth. This, and
the handling of space in general and landscape in particular,
belongs to Eichendorff's most intimate poetic sphere. This conviction is strengthened by two separate observations: on the
one hand, the poet's conception of these scenic and meteorological
values contradicts common Romantic usage and is, on the other,
a constitutive part of his poetic universe. The typically Romantic
convention since Novalis' *Hymnen an die Nacht (Hymns to
Night)* of 1799, extols the night over the day to the point of
religious ecstasy. In the dark or moonlit landscapes where the
contours blur and realities dissolve, the irrational Romantic soul
can take to its flights. Eichendorff's night, in contrast, is profoundly ambiguous. His dreamy young heroes are certainly not
impervious to its magic beauty. As a matter of fact, they are
again and again lured into the silvery expanses of the nocturnal
world. But it is always at the peril of their very souls that they
succumb to its allurement, for magic is both enchanting and
threatening. The night is the time when Eros awakens or, to use
vocabulary consistent with Eichendorff's allegorical language,
when the marble statues in the palatial parks come to life (this
does not occur in *Ahnung und Gegenwart* and is reserved for
later works, such as *Das Marmorbild,* but the principle is already
working in the early novel). This experience is delightful because the Rococo castles and parks remind them of their childhood in the prerevolutionary years, now irretrievably lost; but
it is also dangerous because every statue restored to life is

Venus, the lovely pagan goddess. To lie in her arms and become
her lover would be wonderful, but it would mean the loss of
Christian salvation. Usually, the young hero is saved from yield-
ing at the last moment by "a pious old song" which someone
sings outside. This combination of poetry and Christianity is ordi-
narily sufficient to instill in him the moral strength needed to
withstand the temptation. Eichendorff is perfectly aware of his
deviation from Romantic mythology on this point, for he likes
to satirize the moonstruck Romanticists with their exaggerated
enthusiasm for everything nocturnal. It is these and similar attitudes, announcing an alienation from Romanticism, that have led
to Eichendorff's inclusion among the Biedermeier authors.[39]

Morning is Eichendorff's favorite time of day. He never tires
of its sparkling beauty. Often he leads his heroes to elevated
places where they can survey the marvels of a sunrise, described
in the author's ever recurring formulaic phrases such as "Die
Sonne ging eben prächtig auf" (The sun was just rising magnificently).[40] Of all the allegorical figures he created, Aurora the
goddess of the morning, and the patron saint of chaste love, is
perceptibly closest to his heart. Of course, Eichendorff does not
extol the morning per se. One of the distinguishing marks of his
art is that nothing is seen in isolation. The morning is a symbol
of man's harmony with nature and the visible reflection of his
kinship with the creation. It is in the early morning that the
wanderlust is strongest and that his wanderers joyfully stride
along the roads, singing in competition with the birds.

The opposite can be said of the afternoons when the sun has
gone beyond the zenith and all of creation is languishing in the
sweltering heat of the afternoon. The hour of Pan is an hour of
paralysis. For man it is an hour of deep melancholy when he
realizes that, as a natural creature, he is hopelessly subject to the
indifferent rhythm of up and down, life and death, which is the
law of nature, and he is seized by a great longing for the benefits
of human companionship and social culture. Now he understands
that he is a moral agent.[41] Such is the general meaning Eichendorff attributes to the times of the day; and he conjures them up,
again and again, with never diminishing delight.

Less opposed to Romantic conventions are, at first sight, Eichendorff's preferred elements of landscape, the sailing of the clouds
and the rustling of the leaves, the rivers, the mountains and the

forests, with an occasional French horn thrown in: these are the
fundamental scenic elements with which he builds his innumerable landscapes. It is in *the way* he builds them that he is unique
in the history of German literature. Ingenious studies have been
made of the uncanny simplicity with which Eichendorff creates
space. One of the most perspicacious critics, Richard Alewyn,
has demonstrated how the typical Eichendorff landscape, immediately recognizable as his and nobody else's, is constructed.[42]

Before going on to my own observations about the peculiar
constitution of Eichendorffian space, I wish to summarize Alewyn's findings by quoting the same model passage he used:

Draussen aber ging der herrlichste Sommermorgen funkelnd an allen
Fernstern des Palastes vorüber, alle Vögel sangen in der schönen
Einsamkeit, während von fern aus den Tälern die Morgenglocken
über den Gärten heraufklangen.[43]

But outside, the most wonderful summer morning sparklingly passed
along all the windows of the palace, all the birds were singing in the
beautiful solitude while from afar, out of the valleys, the sound of
the morning bells came up across the garden.

In my translation I have not only tried to be as literal as possible,
but also to retain those peculiarities that give the original its
flavor, even if they sound awkward in English. The passage comes
from the novella "Viel Lärmen um nichts" (Much Ado about
Nothing) but might be found, with identical or similar elements,
in *Ahnung und Gegenwart* or any other of Eichendorff's prose
works. As a matter of fact, it occurs, with slight alterations and
substitutions, a hundred times in his writings—interchangeable
and omissible, and yet of central importance.

Part of the celebrated effect of such landscapes comes from
their position in context. The "but" of the above passage, in con-
junction with the adverb "outside," points to a contrast with a
confined interior[44] (in this particular instance, between the un-
tidy room of the aging Prince Romano, filled with his cosmetic
paraphernalia, and the wide expanse of unspoiled nature). Within the landscape description itself, it is not, as one might expect,
the nouns, that constitute the main linguistic basis. Poetic nonen-
tities, they are merely the ingredients one would find in other
Romantic landscapes, and since Eichendorff often substitutes

more or less equivalent synonyms for each of them, the fundamental structure of the sentences must be insured by other grammatical elements. It is the verbs—to be absolutely precise—the
verbal prefixes, prepositions, and adverbs that make up the
Eichendorffian landscape. The phrase "the most wonderful summer morning . . . passed along the windows," called a "mythical
personification" by Leo Spitzer, adds the dimension of time to the
scenery, puts dynamic movement into it, and contains the cell of
Eichendorff's allegorizing. Light, motion, and space are the real
components of his landscapes. The concrete details are incidental
and rarely even appear as the subjects of his sentences. Let us
observe the repetition of the same grammatical structure elsewhere in the passage: "passed *along*," "came *across*," "*out of* the
valleys" are expressions that add depth and distance.

It has been observed that Eichendorff's sceneries always appear
as being seen from above. We can pinpoint what causes this impression here, namely such adverbial expressions as "out of the
valleys" and "up across the garden," which are invariably slipped
in. A glance at the adjectives reveals that they are so general as
to contain almost no values of perception. The "all" modifying
windows and birds increases rather than defines the vagueness,
and "the most wonderful" of mornings is a value judgment rather
than a sense perception. And so is "beautiful" as an attribute of
"solitude," which, in itself, is a strange word, for it is not used, in
its customary sense, as a psychological condition but as a topographical designation. As such it reinforces two of the impressions
gained so far: that of vagueness and that of expanse.

Still another detail is characteristic of Eichendorff's style: the
acoustic elements added to the expected visual ones. Birds and
bells are not visible ingredients of the picture; they are there because of their capacity for sound. It is interesting to observe how
they are dematerialized and reduced to mere grammatical subjects for their verbs. In the case of the birds this is achieved by
the "all" which distributes the sound all over the space, robbing,
at the same time, the noun of its bodily or visual qualities. A
similar effect is achieved by the definite article accompanying the
morning bells. In both cases, the plural helps to underline the
observations already made. In general, it is striking how many of
the nouns Eichendorff manages to put in the plural, thus contributing to the feeling of scope and distribution. Above all, it is

the "valleys" which create the enormous width of the landscape. The singular is mostly reserved for the objects in the foreground. Thereby, and with the aid of the many directional verb prefixes and spatial prepositions (some of which are difficult to translate into English, such as "an . . . vorüber" or "vorbei," "aus . . . herauf," etc.), Eichendorff's landscape is endowed with a carefully structured perspective. But what is observed by its built-in observer, whose presence coordinates every feature of the landscape, is movement rather than static objects. And the movement, in turn, is that of light and sound across various scenic features, rather than the movement of the objects themselves, which have been largely dematerialized by means of devices already described.

Alewyn employs an ingenious method to impress upon his readers the layered nature of these landscapes by first removing and then replacing those syntactical elements that make up the distance. In our model passage, "while the sound of the morning bells came" would convey little of the magic transmitted by the unmutilated landscape; "while the sounds of the morning bells came up," "while the sound of the morning bells came up across the garden," "while from afar the sounds of the morning bells came up across the garden," "while from afar out of the valleys the sound of the morning bells came up across the garden": this succession restores to our consciousness, one by one, the elements that cause depth and distance.

That these landscapes are structured by the perspective-producing presence of a viewer or listener must not be construed as "subjective" Romanticism. Very unlike the Romantic writers, Eichendorff never uses his landscapes for the reflection or projection of feelings, whether his or those of his characters. What is created by them is space, not feelings—the peculiar space of Eichendorff's world in which even the most conventional happenings are transformed into something poetic or at least into something very much the author's own.

But there is something else about this space to which not enough attention has been paid, but which harbors a strange contradiction. In spite of its great expanses, which we have seen to be built up by a multitude of stylistic features, Eichendorff's space is circumscribed in a fashion that the empirical space of our everyday life is not. In so many instances that to speak of "coincidence" is impossible, the entire world of the protagonist is most implausibly placed within one and the same landscape. Take, for example, the end of *Ahnung und Gegenwart* which, because of its preferred position at the conclusion, cannot be taken lightly. That a final passage in a book carries special weight, that its every word will echo on in the reader's mind long after he has finished the book, are such elementary facts of experience that special care can be assumed to have been employed in its composition.

Friedrich had not noticed any of it. Calmed and blissfully happy, he had stepped out into the quiet garden of the monastery. There he still saw on one side Faber journey out between rivers, vineyards, and blossoming gardens into the flashing, colorfully agitated life; from the other side he saw Leontin's ship with its white sail disappear at the most distant elevation of the ocean between heaven and water. The sun was just rising magnificently.[45]

This paragraph contains a great deal of the space-inducing characteristics we have observed. But in spite of its enormous scope, reaching from horizon to horizon, it holds only the elements necessary for the occasion and no more. This fact makes it shrink spiritually at the very moment when it has achieved an amazing physical extension. The reason is not difficult to find for this is not an ordinary landscape, a part of the world that imposes itself on the view with all its richness and unpredictable detail, but a scene *created by the glance of the viewer* and containing just those phenomena which the author needs for the occasion. Eichendorff's landscape is a stylized, symbolic, metaphysical landscape. Perhaps the most revealing word in the passage is "life." It would not be there were this not the concluding cadence of the novel. Faber, ostensibly taking another of his horseback trips, does not traverse a concrete, well-defined region of this earth, but is going back into *Life*. Leontin, on the other hand, is still adventurous and active and braves the ocean to find his salvation in faraway lands. So perilous, in fact, is his undertaking and so radical his quest that there is nothing between the treacherous element and the heavens but he himself. The puny ship with a single sail is a symbolic translation of the enormity of his enterprise.

Friedrich, as the central figure, supplies the perspective. As every human being must, he occupies the center of his horizon while his friends are on either side. We know what it is that he has ceased to notice: Rosa's, his former beloved's, fainting and departure. For the first time in his career, he is becalmed. Again he steps out from an interior into the open, into freedom. His foreground is the convent garden. All the trouble and turmoil is over, and all mysteries are explained. The sun can rise and illuminate the scene once and for all.

One could naively ask what mountains in Germany these may be (with a monastery on top) from which one can see the ocean on one side, and rivers and vineyards on the other? From what port did ships with no more than a single sail depart for America in the nineteenth century? The only thing to be gained from such pedantic queries is the confirmation that this is not a "real" landscape. The important part is that, with a beautifully allegorical disdain of probability, it once more unites the three friends, the *poeta activus*, the *poeta contemplativus*, and the *poeta faber* (for poets they are, above all) in the same suggestive space.

The idea that certain meanings which require our interpretation are contained in a landscape has been expressed by Eichendorff himself more than once. At one point in *Ahnung und Gegenwart*, the author has Friedrich express it in these words: "How true it is that inherent in every region is a beauty characteristic to it alone, a special idea which seeks to express itself with its brooks, trees, and mountains, as if with inarticulate words. He whom these individual sounds move will fit together the whole discourse with few means."[46] This is reminiscent of the Romantic passion of seeing nature as a hieroglyph. Other pronouncements suggest that Eichendorff had something of this sort in mind. At the same time, however, the passage contains a clue as to how he conceived of landscape and how he wanted us to read the ones he himself created.

These observations may also serve to consolidate our impressions of Eichendorff's relationship to reality. What are we to make of two riverboats weaving so closely in and out of their paths that every facial expression and every detail about the passengers can be clearly observed from one ship to the other? Or of a promenade on the river bank, also observed from a passing vessel, with ladies and gentlemen in their Sunday best, greeting and bowing to each other, and accompanied by gay music? Is this an example of Eichendorff's utter disregard for probability, or do we have to look for another explanation? (In this particular case, both occurrences referred to are part of the opening allegory. The two ships are the "ships of life" of Friedrich and Rosa—as if confirmation were necessary, Faber says "Das Reisen ist dem Leben vergleichbar" [Traveling is comparable to life][47], and the promenade is supposed to signify the gay, but superficial intercourse of the sexes.) And how are we supposed to react to the fact that the Residence, hardly spoken of until that time, becomes visible from the next hill when it is on Rosa's mind?[48] Or to the fact that Rosa herself, when Friedrich is thinking of her, immediately appears riding in the distance, unattainable but phenomenally present in the landscape?[49]

The examples for juxtaposing disparate elements of scenery (symbolic of opposing spiritual spheres—such as Baron von A.'s country estate and the residential capital[50]) which happen to find their common denominator solely in the mental processes of the protagonists, are so frequent that they defy enumeration. Nor is there any need for it. From the material already adduced, the conclusion can be drawn that Eichendorff's world is extensive and full of delightful detail, but not infinite or representative of independent empirical space. Eichendorff's "what is" comprises a total "reality," and not only our world of sense data. The dense carpet of our sense perceptions is in his fiction but a transparent film spread over an ultimate truth. He does not bother to account for its individual traits too closely. Many of them seem identical with the ones of which our own world is composed. But our deception lasts only for a moment. For Eichendorff combines them in an arbitrary fashion—not duplicated in the normal world —to form beautiful patterns for his own purpose. And even this must not be regarded as his final aim. What he really wants to accomplish with his veil is, by making it as delicate as possible, to let shine through what is underneath it. What Eichendorff is after is not beauty but truth.

V   *Poetry and Poets*

The previously quoted poem about a song slumbering in all things and the magic word that is capable of awakening it[51] betrays Eichendorff's belief in the animation of all things, a kind of pantheism which he did not always find easy to reconcile with Christianity. It also states that poetry is a supreme tool of cognition. What later poets, theoretically more conscious and more articulate (such as Rilke), said about their *Dinggedichte* is already expressed here, albeit in simplified form. Unconscious or semi-conscious creation needs the poet as a mouthpiece. It depends on him, its noblest embodiment, for expression. But only the poet close to creation and in possession of a magic key can render this service. The result is the poem. In it, poet and world, self and other, individual and cosmos become one. It is the philosophy of life of a lyricist.

Some of these views stand behind the many conversations about poetry presented in *Ahnung und Gegenwart*. This is how Leontin expresses Eichendorff's basic conviction about the poetic nature of the world. "Life," he says, "with its many-colored pictures, is in relation to the poet as an immensely complex book of hieroglyphs in an unknown protolanguage, long since vanished, is to a reader."[52] It is characteristic of Eichendorff's novels that all the major characters are practicing poets, each representing a particular attitude toward poetry. While both Leontin and Friedrich are expressive of some aspects of Eichendorff's mind, Leontin is the more skeptical, unruly, and irrational of the two. It is in this light that we must understand the words with which he complements the above statement: "The most honest, the most good-natured fools of the world, the poets, sit there from eternity to eternity and read and read. But the ancient, wondrous words behind these symbols are unknown, and the wind blows the pages of the great book so rapidly and so confusedly back and forth that one's vision gets blurred."[53] It is Friedrich who is the author's mouthpiece in his more pious moods (not only in matters poetic) and he is therefore called upon to contradict Leontin's extreme views. In terms of Eichendorff's poetics *in nuce,* Leontin has been saying: A song slumbers in all things, all right. But who can decipher it? It is Friedrich's task to assert the second half: The world will sing if you find the magic word. "In contrast to the lazy crowd intent upon nothing but worldly things, the poet alone," he says, "keeps his beautiful eyes open; in humility and joy he regards, himself amazed, heaven and earth. His heart goes out to the overwhelming view and thus he sings about the world which will resound . . . full of silent meaning only when touched by the Aurora of a poetic soul with its

kindred rays."[54] Friedrich, like Eichendorff, sees poetry in a
religious and—to be even more exact—in a Christian role: "The
holy martyrs, leaping into the lethal flames with outstretched
arms, loudly professing their Saviour—these are the true brothers
of the poet."[55] Now we understand better what "a poetic soul"
is, and what it takes to express the creation in poetry: Christian
faith.

The conversation in which these exchanges take place occurs
early in the novel, and it is Faber's, the professional poet's views
that are likely to appeal to the modern reader. "To be poetic and
to be a poet are two very different things," he opines. "In the
case of the latter . . . there is always some sleight of hand, acro-
batics, etc. involved."[56] This sounds very much like Thomas
Mann (and is, of course, taken from Goethe). And a moment
before he has formulated an insight about poetry that Rilke could
have written:[57] "You think that writing poetry is such an easy
thing because the words flow easily from the pen; but no one
considers that a child, conceived in pleasure perhaps many years
ago, must be nourished and shaped in the mother's womb with
joys and pains before it can greet the gay light of day from its
quiet house."[58] But these views are rejected. They are too reminis-
cent of the poetics of Enlightenment, with its stress of experience,
the rational processes of the mind, and the importance of deliberate craftsmanship.

The startling thing is not that Eichendorff should have little
use for a theory of this kind, but how accurately and sympathetically he represents it and that Faber remains an ambiguous figure
to the very end, with as many admirable traits as ludicrous ones.
He is one of the few characters of Eichendorff's about whom
the reader is allowed to make up his own mind. We are probably
not far from the truth if we see a Goethe figure in him.[59] To
portray Goethe in their novels had become a pastime for the
German Romantics since Novalis' *Heinrich von Ofterdingen*
(1800), and the idea of linking the father of modern German
literature with a representation of the *poeta faber* would not
be a far-fetched one even if Faber himself were not to invoke
the sage's authority in support of his poetic theories: "As our
great master Goethe himself confesses."[60]

The ambiguity surrounding Faber originates with the moment
of his appearance. "Friedrich was very startled by this name," is

the central character's first reaction. "He had read a great deal by Faber; some of his things he had not liked at all, but many others had so moved him that he could not comprehend how the same man had been able to create such beauty."[61] The curious thing, from our modern point of view, is that Friedrich is made out to be an observant realist, whereas Faber's fault lies in a purely esthetic cult of beauty and concomitant lack of moral conviction. But we must remember that this is exactly the light in which the aging Goethe appeared to the youngest generation: as a man unable to commit himself to any ideal, be it social or national. Goethe was over sixty-five when *Ahnung und Gegenwart* appeared.

These passages will be more meaningful to present-day readers when seen in the light of the age-old battle between *l'art pour l'art* and an engaged literature. To illustrate the discrepancy between his esthetics and his moral stance, Faber is made to read a glowing patriotic romance entitled "To the Germans," in which an allegorical knight, in spite of dying from his many wounds, defies all the enemies of German honor. His listeners are considerably edified by the virility of these sentiments. But Leontin recalls with amazement that, at the time of writing the poem, Faber fled ignominiously to avoid fighting the French, whereupon Faber pulls from his pocket another poem in which he ridicules his own cowardice.[62] He sensibly argues against "confusing life and poetry,"[63] but is refuted by one of Friedrich's moralistic sermons: "How do you expect people to esteem your works, to be refreshed and uplifted by them, if you yourself do not believe what you are writing and try to outwit God and men by beautiful words and artful thoughts?"[64] No doubt, Friedrich does not share Faber's views. But he is forced again and again to admire his poetry and like him as a person. Phrases such as "Friedrich found him very lovable at this moment" are calculated to keep the question of Faber indeterminate. In a rousing statement on poetry, Friedrich works himself into a frenzy of righteous rhetoric so that, when he finishes, Leontin embraces him enthusiastically and even Faber agrees: "Beautifully said, particularly toward the end," so that one might assume the controversy settled. But it is precisely Faber's comment which proves him to be the incorrigible estheticist who observes a rhetorical effect when his friend is pouring out his soul. And thus Friedrich concludes correctly: "None of them mean it as I do."[65]

The interesting thing about Friedrich's poetics is that it is not only directed against an empiricist-rationalist philosophy like that of Faber, but also contains statements obviously critical of Romantic esthetics as well. "I absolutely loathe those ceaseless complaints whimpering about the good old times in tearful sonnets,"[66] he says. Leontin's self-mockery about his former belief that he himself was the "world soul" and that because of so much world he no longer knew whether or not he had a soul at all,[67] reinforces the same point. These statements must be construed as Eichendorff's criticism of certain maudlin tendencies in Romanticism and philosophical idealism. Remarks about poetry and poets are interspersed everywhere. But it is in Book Two that Eichendorff dwells at length, in the negative form of satire, on the nature of contemporary literature, which is portrayed as a major symptom of the general corruption.[68]

One of the most effective devices of Eichendorff's satire is that of incongruity. We are prepared for the application of this method to literary matters in Book One. Friedrich and Leontin overhear a dialogue between two literarily inclined lovers.[69] " 'Did you read the newest work by Lafontaine?'[70] asks the young man. 'Yes,' the girl replies, 'I read it, my noble friend! and it elicited my tears, tears which any feeling person is glad to shed!' " The verbal exchange continues in this tone for quite some time and culminates in a frenzy of beautiful sentiments. "O holy melancholy," the young man exclaims, "thou sympathetic harmony of attuned souls. Our love is as pure as the moon up there!" At the same time, however, "he began to work frantically on the girl's bodice, encountering only little resistance." Leontin, in his hideout, only states the obvious: "Now they have relapsed into their true nature, and the devil has fetched their poetry."

This is satire by coarse contrast, and much of Book Two is based on the same principle. The discussions and recitations in the literary salon are discredited by the clash of a pretended spirituality and erotic interest only imperfectly concealed behind it. Not only is there a "secret understanding" between the hostess and one of the satirized poets, called "Der Schmachtende" (the languisher)—in Eichendorff's vocabulary a synonym for "trivial Romanticist"—but at the same time she manages to begin "ein

feines Liebäugeln" (refined ogling)[71] that seemed intended for
Friedrich himself.

Another discrepancy, satirically exploited by Eichendorff, is the
one betwen semblance and reality that permeates the entire
scene. The hostess herself turns out to be "much slyer than one
would have initially thought compatible with her lisping gentleness; she seemed to ignore her languishing lover and, in a most
enlightened manner, seemed to think less of him than she pretended and he believed from the bottom of his soul."[72]

The tension between pretending and feeling is characteristic
for the whole tone prevailing in the salon. One of its social lions
"suddenly turned to the languishing gentleman with very vehe-
ment pleas to read them a few more of his excellent sonnets,
although, as Friedrich had perfectly well overheard, he had made
these very poems the targets of his wit and mockery in front of
the ladies."[73] The purpose of the entire chapter[74] is, no doubt,
to build up the contrast between this "heartless, double-dealing
devilishness" and Friedrich's Old-German honesty. When he
dislikes something, he does not mince words but resolutely
proclaims, "I do not like your poems at all."[75] No wonder that he
is the cause for the untimely collapse of the literary soirée. "What
holds the whole thing tolerably together are a thousand delicate,
almost invisible threads of vanity, praise and counter-praise, etc.,
which they are very fond of calling a golden net of love. But if
someone who knows nothing about it moves around in it vigor-
ously and unexpectedly, the whole spider web of eternal friendship and holy alliance falls apart. That is exactly how Friedrich
spoiled the whole tea. No one was able to get the artistic shut-
tle, which was normally weaving in perfect rhythm the tenderest
esthetic evenings, going again. Most people became ill-humored;
as in the case of the tower of Babel, no one wanted or was able
to understand the other's verbal fireworks, and so one offended
the other in this total confusion."[76] This is a typical case, deliberately framed by Eichendorff, of the clumsy but pure-hearted
German elephant wreaking havoc in the porcelain shop of false
polite society.

One is never at a loss as to the meaning of Eichendorff's satirical sallies. Obligingly he always proffers his explicit comments.
One of the salon sages who holds the ladies spellbound with
his oracular pronouncements is not so much discredited by what

he says—for we are not made conversant with his opinions—but by the comment with which Eichendorff accompanies his never-quoted bon mots: "He really did not belong to any one party; he surveyed them all from afar and smiled about the opposing views and endeavors, the zealous dispute among philosophers or poets: he felt himself to be the highlight of these various reflexes."[77] Another salon prophet, "whose face shimmered and beamed with smug complacency," is condemned by means of depreciatory physiognomical attributes such as "bursting with health" and a "penetrating, shrill voice."[78] The poem which he reads with such great effort that his "face turned all blue," is dismissed as a "dithyramb about God, heaven, hell, earth, and the carbuncle."[79] The fairest treatment is accorded the third of the three literati portrayed as the representatives of the capital's cultural life, because the poems he is reading to the assembled audience are actually quoted. Of course, "his sweetly pouched mouth" and certain disgusting snatches of his conversation do not bode well for him. But the products of his Muse are reproduced verbatim and the reader is permitted to judge for himself. Or is he? The poor, ill-advised man, instead of contenting himself with a simple *Lied*-like poem about marble statues, stage coaches, forests, and French horns, chooses to entertain us, inveterate Eichendorff readers that we are, with a rhythmically elaborate poem in Spanish assonances, the first stanza of which reads:

> Hat nun Lenz die silbern'n Bronnen
>   Losgebunden:
> Knie ich nieder, süss beklommen
> In die Wunder.

> Spring has now the silver wells
>   untied:
> Down I kneel, sweetly oppressed
> Into the miracles.

Not quite satisfied yet, he adds a sonnet about love, kneeling, and heaven, and, in Eichendorff's own words, "he still read a whole pile of sonnets with a kind of priestly solemnity."[80] We already suspect that the religious sentiments expressed in these poems will do little to raise him in Friedrich's or Eichendorff's

estimation. Why did he have to present them in sonnets which
Eichendorff considered, at least in *Ahnung und Gegenwart,* an
artificial, un-German form? But lest we be deceived by the
residue of poetry in them, the existence of which he readily
concedes, Eichendorff supplies us with a full analysis of these
artifacts. They were not, we are informed, totally devoid of
sincere feeling, grandiose expressions, and lovely images. But
while dealing with the divine nature of poetry, "poetry itself,
spontaneous, free, and robust life, which grips us before we
speak about it, remained hidden behind all the compliments and
preparations for it."[81] In these sentences, the rock of positive
belief from which the scenery is satirically surveyed, enters into
view. A sweeping dismissal of the entire literary congregation
concludes with these judgments: "These poetizers, in their thoroughly polished, flamboyant, well-bred effeminacy, seemed to
Friedrich like the insipid, disagreeable tea vapors, the dainty
teapot with its flaming alcohol on the table, the sacrificial altar
of these Muses."[82]

The scene is a strange mixture of pedantic moralizings and
disarming humor. At any rate, to write a whole poem in a style
which is to be condemned a moment later, is a delightful satirical
trick and, in a poet so young and inexperienced as Eichendorff
at the time, a proof of wit and versatility. That he manages to
satirize the social and cultural life of his epoch in one literary
soirée adds complexity to his novel. What incensed him especially
was a literary fad, a trend in post-Romantic poetry, which con-
sisted of an ostentation of sentimental Christian piety. Nothing
could have angered young Eichendorff, who was genuinely
religious, more than esthetic bantering with religion. It is, therefore, not unusual for him to condense his attitude in an allegory
that precedes the description of the entire gathering. Reference
has already been made to a tableau in which the Countess
Romana represented Venus. Suggestively illuminated by the
moon, the guests at the soirée represented the following scene:
A female figure raises a cross to heaven with one hand, while
clasping her heart with the other. She is surrounded by dreamlike plants and animals. Below, a kneeling knight, leaning on his
sword, fully faces this image of Christian Glory, while a figure
of Venus, frightened by what delights him, is half turned away.

Friedrich is, of course, deeply moved by what he sees. When-

ever Eichendorff uses the word "Aurora," we are entitled to
suspect religious emotion, and here we read that "in his breast
the power of joyous, lofty resolutions and thoughts was kindled;
the evening glow outside was for him the Aurora of a wide
and wonderful life to come, and his whole soul flew as though
on large wings into the marvelous sight."[83] But how do the
others react to this tableau which transports Friedrich, as it
were, into another world? In the middle of his rapture, the
curtain falls, the chandelier is lowered, and "cackling bustle and
laughter suddenly filled the room again."[84] What had been a
religious experience for him was, at best, an esthetic stimulus
for the others. This is the gist of Eichendorff's quarrel with the
contemporary world. At this stage of his development, he is still
accustomed to translate into grammatical discourse what he has
already expressed in imagery, and thus Friedrich once more puts
into plain words what he thinks of the esthetic use of Christian
symbols: "Hardly have we gotten rid of rationalizing in matters
of religion, when we already begin again to poeticize and vola-
tilize its firm dogmas, miracles, and truths. He in whom religion
comes to life, who is truly inspired by Grace in all his activities,
may express his soul in songs and enjoy the ecstasies of religion
and the heavenly radiance in this fashion. But he who thinks he
can arrogantly and cleverly dispose of the mysteries and simple
truths as mere poetic subject matter, who merely with the imagination gathers the individual beauties of religion—which does
not belong to faith, to reason, or to poetry alone, but to all three,
to the whole man—will just as willingly believe in the Greek
Olympus as in Christianity and confuse and substitute one for the
other, until the whole heaven becomes an empty and desolate
place."[85]

The passage had to be quoted *in extenso* because it is not
only a wholesale indictment of the intellectual fashion in Eichendorff's day, but a succinct statement of his own philosophy of life
and the role of poetry in it. To these insights nothing new is
added in the course of the novel. Only toward the end, when
everything imperiously hastens toward a solution, Faber raises
one more point about poetry: the question of its fate in a life
dedicated to the pursuit of religion. This passage, too, is worth
quoting at length. After Friedrich has expounded his reasons
for retreating from the depravity of the world into a monastery

and fighting for a more propitious future from the bastion of its peaceful precincts, Faber once more propounds his view of poetry as an esthetic force unencumbered by ideological commitments: As you spoke," he reflects, "I had an odd feeling as if poetry and all art were disappearing in the most distant of distances, and as if I had lost my life to a charming trifle. For poetry's aiming toward the outside, the mental preoccupation and concern with what is going on at a given moment, the struggle with, and intervention in, the times, great as it may be as an attitude, is basically inartistic. Poetry may take root in the same ground as religion and nationality, but without ulterior purpose, to grow up toward us as a wondrous flower for the sake of its heavenly beauty alone."[86]

As is so often the case in this novel, Friedrich replies, in the form of a lengthy poem, defending his position and asserting the compatibility of seclusion from the world with the continued existence of poetry. The key stanza, whose concluding line has become a catchword in Eichendorff criticism, runs as follows:

> Der Dichter kann nicht mit verarmen;
> Wenn alles um ihn her zerfällt,
> Hebt ihn ein göttliches Erbarmen—
> Der Dichter ist das Herz der Welt.

> The poet cannot be impoverished;
> If everything around him falls apart,
> Divine mercy upholds him—
> The poet is the heart of the world.

Faber remains true to himself. In one of the last images employed in the novel, Eichendorff sends forth Faber, unconvinced and unconverted, into the "flashing, gaily agitated life" without which his kind of poetry cannot flourish. As far as Eichendorff himself is concerned, the image proves that he was at least as great a poet as he was an ideologist.

VI *Weltanschauung*

Eichendorff's cultural pessimism in *Ahnung und Gegenwart* extends to every aspect of society. But with the exception of the loose sexual mores and the literary activities in the capital, there are few areas of life which he singles out for analysis. Toward the end of Book One, in a scene set at the country estate of Baron von A., he records a verbal exchange between Friedrich and Julie's aunt on the subject of the most suitable education for a young lady of the landed gentry. It is by no means unexpected that "natural" simplicity and avoidance of the false sophistication of the modern methods are advocated. A product of her own generation and receptive to what is "fashionable," the aunt entertains vague notions about "enlightenment, *Bildung*, genteel manners" and regrets not having sent Julie to what she calls "a house of education" in the capital where young women learn the je-ne-sais-quoi indispensable in social life. Obviously, she has in mind a finishing school for daughters of the upper classes. To those who are, by now, familiar with Friedrich's character, it cannot come as a surprise that this talk provokes one of his earnest lectures with a strong admixture of self-righteous morality. He expressly states "that country life is best for young ladies." In the famous city institutions, "vanity and a disastrous obsession with imitation levels out and corrupts the childlike originality of every girl."[87] Julie's own role as the sole feminine success of the novel and what we are later shown of city education bear out in practice Friedrich's theoretical postulates.

These discussions about matters of culture and philosophy belong to the heritage of the Goethean *Entwicklungsroman* (developmental novel) after which *Ahnung und Gegenwart* is largely patterned. But much as Eichendorff's conversations remind the historical-minded reader of *Wilhelm Meisters Lehrjahre* they also readily reveal their inadequacy in context. Goethe's cultural disquisitions are always full of carefully observed detail and intellectual penetration, entirely absorbed by the design of character and plot, whereas Eichendorff's lack these dimensions of observation and integration. Usually, two modes of thinking, one attributed to contemporary society and another expressed by Eichendorff's docile protagonists, are pitted against one another. There is never a doubt as to who is right, and the result is rather two-dimensional. What the author objects to in the products of city education holds true of many of his own opinions: that they are immediately recognizable "by their well-bred propriety," and that one often knows beforehand "what kind of witticism or joke will follow, what their favorite disposition will be."[88] Clearly,

the chief value of *Ahnung und Gegenwart* is not intellectual;
nor is it possible to regard the work as a true *Bildungsroman,*
a novel of education and development, no matter how closely
it may resemble one in its external form.

The treatment of politics in Book Two of the novel is no
exception to the aforesaid. Although involvement in politics
changes the hero's course of life and precipitates his final adoption
of the monastic ideal, very little concrete detail is given. Allusions
to "the frightening march of the times" and "the false poets . . .
who, unmindful of the tremendous admonitions of the epoch,
squandered their national strength in idle poetic play,"[89] are
veiled references to the Napoleonic question. In contrast to the
idle poets, Friedrich's youthful dream of "the marvelous minstrel
from the mountain of Venus changed into a holy love and enthusiasm for the definite and firm purpose"[90] which, we must
assume, is that of national liberation. Lured by the handsome,
but unstable Prince, Friedrich joins a political group, "a fine
circle of new, vigorous friends who . . . had come together from
various German regions, . . . working industriously, hoping and
trusting that they would make room for the old law in these
oppressive times, resolved for life and death."[91] That is all one
learns about the political orientation and the concrete goals of
this loose association.

The skeptical Leontin sees through what he calls this "comedy,"
the success of which he predicts to be the greater the more often
the word "German" appears.[92] He proves to be right. When the
war breaks out, the friends of this circle have long since dis-
persed. "With the coming of spring they forgot seriousness,
honesty, and their common endeavors, together with the balls and
other winter amusements." Indeed, one of them is captured by
Friedrich's troops as a member of the enemy forces. When up-
braided for his treason, he tries to kill Friedrich. The hero is
the only one to remain true to the cause. Judging by the proximity to Italy, the mountainous region in which he meets them, and
an occasional dialect word they use, it is the Tyrolese rebels
against Napoleon in whose company he chooses to fight the
enemy of the nation. The war is lost and, his Prince having
chosen the other side, Friedrich is proscribed, and his castle and
possessions confiscated.

If we translate the novelistic terms in which these happenings

are related into the language of history, it is possible to recon-
struct the following sequence of events: The residence in which
Book Two is set, represents one of those independent German
principalities which allowed anti-Napoleonic movements to de-
velop but at the critical moment chose to ally themselves with the
likely victor. Not surprisingly, Eichendorff, himself a participant
in the wars of liberation between the conception and publication
of *Ahnung und Gegenwart,* adds a lack of consistent nationalism
to the register of sins incurred by his epoch. Long before the
reader is even led to the "Residenz," he is given, in characteristic
Eichendorffian anticipation, a summary of what it stands for in
the novel. Shortly after Rosa has left for the capital, the scene
of her future life and downfall becomes visible to the friends
in the distance, and Friedrich comments: "Do you see the dark
spires of the Residence? They stand erect like the gravestones of
the day that has just set. The people there, among whom Rosa
will now move, are different; true morals, piety, and simplicity
are valueless for them."[93]

It was Spengler who said "culture is city culture." If he is
right, Eichendorff is condemning the entire culture of his times.
Its epitaph, reflecting the author's social point of view, is again
placed in Friedrich's mouth: "God help the nobility."[94]

Ahnung und Gegenwart is a cyclical novel. It derives its whole
momentum from a return to old values—old Christianity, old
chivalry, and the old way of life—and a rejection of everything
new.[95] All of these ideas are expressed directly and unequivocally
and could easily be transferred to any of Eichendorff's cultural-
historical essays. But the philosophy of return is also contained
in a deeper linguistic sphere, i.e., the imagery of the novel. In
this realm it is the wholeness of childhood to which the characters
long to return. Not until he has found the companion of his childhood, his lost brother Rudolf who is able to shed light on the
various unexplained mysteries, can Friedrich make the resolution
that is to bring clarity into his own life.

With the war lost, deprived of his possessions, the beautiful
castles where their former life took place in ruins, and Rosa
corrupted, the scene is prepared for the hero's withdrawal to the
monastery. It is, of course, he who, in summarizing the personal,
national, poetic, and religious questions that have been touched

upon, expresses the philosophy of life underlying *Ahnung und Gegenwart:*

There seems to me, in this misery, no other resort than religion. For where is there, in this flood of poetry, piety, Germanity, virtue, and chauvinism which are humming back and forth unsteadily in the present Babylonian confusion, where is there a safe center whence all this could be brought to a clear understanding and formed into a living whole? . . . It is in this conviction that I remain in Germany and choose the cross as my sword. For truly, just as in former times missionaries were sent to the cannibals, this is even more necessary in Europe, the most developed seat of paganism of them all.[96]

CHAPTER 3

The Lyrics

EICHENDORFF'S strength as a poet lies in the realm of lyrical poetry.[1] Even the effectiveness of his prose, which has poems scattered throughout, as we have seen, lies partly in its lyrical qualities. But this does not fully account for Eichendorff's popularity in the German-speaking world. He is considered by many to be the best poet of German Romanticism (and the most pleasant, the freshest, and "healthiest" as well), a movement renowned for its lyrical poetry; moreover, for millions of his compatriots, Eichendorff's stanzas resembling folk songs have represented, for one hundred and fifty years, the fulfillment per se of poetic potential. His *Lieder,* set to music time and again, are sung everywhere. Indeed, some of them have become such an integral part of the standard repertory that composer and poet have been forgotten and word and melody alone are passed on from one generation to the next in veritable immortality, shaping people's conceptions of what poetry should be like. This at least applies up to World War II, the repercussions of which have wrought as yet incalculable changes in the patterns of thinking and the value system of the Germans. Our task will be to seek an explanation for Eichendorff's compelling magnetism, which is felt by simple people as much as by those steeped in literature.

Eichendorff's poetry is distinguished by its diversity and, at the same time, by its astonishing unity, which enables the most untutored reader to identify a poem as being his. Short, proverb-like stanzas and long epic-narrative romances, poems that lend themselves to song and poems with an entire cast of characters, ballads and humorous sketches, dedicatory poems and contemplative poetry belong to the catalogue of his repertory. Eichendorff was less inventive in verse and stanza forms than some of his contemporaries and successors, who delighted in experiment. Nonetheless, he employs a number of poetic measures, long and short metrical lines, the most varied rhythms, all types of German rhyme patterns, and ingenious Spanish assonances. Classical verse and strophic measures are missing, but variations of the *terza rima* and the sonnet appear in abundance.

Eichendorff's preference for a few topics, however, somewhat narrows this diversity. Endeavoring to survey the thematic material treated by the Romantic poets, we do not find that Eichendorff had a particularly limited scope; still a certain conventionality of his subjects cannot be denied. Poetry of nature, hunting, soldier, and drinking songs, poems dealing with questions of religion and poetic life, *Wanderlieder* and love songs— be it of love that is joyful or betrayed, unrequited or melancholy —this is, by and large, the substance of Eichendorff's lyrical production. In his day, all of this already belonged to the familiar thematic storehouse of German poetry, which may, to some extent, explain the acclaim accorded his poems. Eichendorff was the heir and masterful exponent of a tradition which had already penetrated all levels of the population.

Further contributing to his popularity is the easy comprehensibility of his poetic message. As an example, let us look at a poem in which we soon will rediscover the problems dealt with in his prose writings. Here the three forces of prime concern for Eichendorff are lyrically fused in a most admirable fashion. The two opening stanzas serve to pose the problem.

DIE ZWEI GESELLEN[2]

Es zogen zwei rüst'ge Gesellen
Zum erstenmal von Haus,
So jubelnd recht in die hellen,
Klingenden, singenden Wellen
Des vollen Frühlings hinaus.

Die strebten nach hohen Dingen,
Die wollten, trotz Lust und Schmerz,
Was Recht's in der Welt vollbringen,
Und wem sie vorüber gingen,
Dem lachten Sinnen und Herz.—

THE TWO COMPANIONS

Two stalwart fellows set forth
From home for the first time,
Jubilantly into the bright
Ringing singing waves
Of the full spring.

They aimed at lofty goals,
They wanted, come joy or pain,
To accomplish something in the world,
And whomever they met in passing
Was gladdened in spirit and heart.

The meaning of these lines is obvious enough to need no lengthy commentary. However, for the reader who wants to become adept at discerning the characteristic features of Eichendorff's lyrical poetry, a few observations may be added. Attention should first be given to the narrative or—technically speaking—ballad-esque tone, which is part and parcel of Eichendorff's poetic style and even leaves its traces on the purely *Lied*-like creations which are more trenchantly imbued with the magic of lyrical enchantment than the poem here considered; for example the famous poems "Mondnacht" ("Es war, als hätt' der Himmel/Die Erde still geküsst" [It was as if the heaven/Had gently kissed the earth]) and "Sehnsucht" (Es schienen so golden die Sterne [So golden shone the stars])—which will be more carefully analyzed.

Typical for this balladesque tone, which can take other forms of expression as well, is the impersonal "es" (it) opening our poem in the original. It immediately suggests epic breadth and an expansive narrative attitude, as in the stock introduction to German fairytales: "Es war einmal" (Once upon a time). That we are on the right track with this comparison is confirmed by the tense of the verb which, in contrast to the classical tense of lyrical poetry, the timeless present, appears in the imperfect— "zogen" (set forth)—thereby producing a reportorial and epic distance. We may add to this a certain grammatical clumsiness, such as the anaphorically-applied "die" (these) (admittedly in keeping with the colloquial tone). Such demonstrative pronouns, replacing the expected relative pronouns and verbal inversion, create in German the impression of simpleminded, awkward honesty. This is joined by a logical construction such as "wem-dem" in the ninth and tenth lines and the fact that the first and second stanzas each consist of one single, irreproachably struc-tured grammatical sentence.

To be sure, the sobering effect which such syntactical details might have is counterbalanced by two additional stylistic touches, the folk-song tone and the genuinely lyrical element. Reminis-cent of folk songs are the apostrophic forms in "rüst'ge Gesellen" and "was Recht's," as are the homespun, standard phrases, such as "so . . . recht" or "Dem lachten Sinnen und Herz" (with the incorrect plural ending). The essentially lyrical component is concentrated in three lines—the third, fourth, and fifth of the first stanza—which suffice to plunge the reader into the core of Eichendorff's metaphorical vocabulary. A sensitive reader, even though still unaware that in Eichendorff the spring is a cipher for the allurement of vegetative life, will immediately be alerted by the intensive orchestration of this stanza. The frequency of liquids (jube*l*nd, he*ll*en, k*l*ingenden, We*ll*en, vo*ll*en, Früh*l*ings), the string of adjectives, the dactylic internal rhyme "klingenden-singenden," the water metaphor (for Eichendorff, water is the treacherous element *par excellence),* the suggestion of vegetative opulence achieved by the unorthodox noun-attribute combination of "voller Frühling"—all of these ingredients make up the linguis-tic correlate to the overpowering seduction the poet wishes to depict. With this the first lyrical climax is reached, a height from which the second stanza, with its assertions about a certain set of goals in life, appears slightly ironical: "Die strebten nach hohen Dingen" (They aimed at lofty goals), etc. The two final lines of this stanza, with their allusion to the expectations which society places in the two youths, lead into the following three stanzas, in which their diverging—in fact, contrary—fates are depicted. Stanza three is devoted to one of them:

> Der erste, der fand ein Liebchen,
> Die Schwieger kauft' Hof und Haus;
> Der wiegte gar bald ein Bübchen
> Und sah aus heimlichem Stübchen
> Behaglich ins Feld hinaus.
>
> The first, he found a sweetheart,
> Her mother bought farm and house,

> Soon he was rocking a baby,
> And snug in his homely parlor,
> He serenely gazed at the fields.

In order to cram an entire life chronicle into five verses, the poet uses such loaded expressions as "Schwieger" (mother-in-law), "Hof und Haus" (farm and house), as well as the rhyming diminutives "Liebchen," "Bübchen," and "Stübchen," (dear sweetheart, wee boy, little parlor), thereby stressing the close relationship between the three. Whoever approaches this poem without some knowledge of Eichendorff's philosophy of life and, therefore, does not automatically register the stock image of the Philistine as it emerges from these lines, will nonetheless surmise, from certain logical indications, the deprecatory tendency underlying this depiction. For the adjectives "heimlich" (homely, in the sense of domestic comfort) and "behaglich" (cozy, snug), and the entire idyllic picture of love and family suggested by "Liebchen," "wiegen," and "Bübchen" don't necessarily have to be negatively evaluated in *every* concept of humanity. However, the "rüst'ge Geselle" (stalwart fellow) doesn't earn his possessions but receives them free of charge from his mother-in-law. The whole throbbing allure of demonic nature in the first stanza has become a field, most likely tilled, to which one relates passively as a (seated) observer from the comfortable confines of the homestead; and, most important, in contrast to the first stanza, the dulcet contentment cannot be interpreted as "striving for higher goals" by any philosophy, no matter how domestically it is disposed. All this, then, indubitably proves that the first fellow has evaded the challenge of spring, its captivating telluric forces, but he has had nothing of equal substance to oppose to it.

While Eichendorff devotes only one stanza to domestic bliss as the solution to the problems of life, he needs two to describe the opposite, thereby illustrating its priority:

> Dem zweiten sangen und logen
> Die tausend Stimmen in Grund,
> Verlockend' Sirenen, und zogen
> Ihn in der buhlenden Wogen
> Farbig klingenden Schlund.
>
> Und wie er auftaucht' vom Schlunde,
> Da war er müde und alt,

Sein Schifflein das lag im Grunde,
So still war's rings in die Runde,
Und über die Wasser weht's kalt.

The second was wooed by songs and lies
Of a thousand voices in the bottom,
Enticing sirens, and drawn down
Into the voluptuous billows
Of the colorful, ringing abyss.

And when he emerged again,
He was tired and old,
His little boat lay at the bottom,
Stillness was all around,
And over the water it blows cold.

In the analysis of literary works, one can never place too much emphasis on details. In poems that are closely structured, every element of form gains power to express content, and every detail of the vocabulary, of the system of metaphors, the structure, and the sound qualities corresponds to a semantic value. It seems as if the poet, by limiting himself to one stanza in the first instance, in contrast to the second, wished to emphasize that there was not much to report about the first fellow. By turning domestic and shallow too soon, he has missed the good life. This case condemns itself, as it were. Of much greater significance is the other extreme—abandoning oneself, "submerging" in spring—as we see not only in the expansiveness with which the poet depicts this possibility but also in the fact that he now returns to the lyrical keynote of the poem, to the music and water metaphors of the first stanza.

The "Stimmen" (voices), the reiteration of the words "Singen" (singing) and "Klingen" (ringing), like the "Wogen" (billows) synonymous with the intial "Wellen" (waves), again raise the subject of spring; only this time the tone has become much more urgent and ominous, for the singing is coupled with "logen" (lies) and the voices that sing have swelled to "one thousand." Now the nature of water as a treacherous, perfidious element becomes unmistakably concrete in the choice of "Grund" (bottom) and "Schlund" (abyss), whose rhyming alone indicates their connection. To the acoustic and tactile sensations a visual one has been added, namely the adjective "farbig" (colorful), which, together with "bunt" (many-colored), is Eichendorff's favorite designation for the magical, sensual diversity of the world. It is also highly significant that the ensnarement is intensified by the appearance of the power of eroticism (the adjective "buhlend," derived from the verbal root "buhlen," which can mean licentiousness as well as courtly wooing, conjures up, as no other word could, the turbulent, forbidden sexuality involved). Finally, all the components—musical, sensual, and enticing—of primitive strength and foreboding of death are masterfully personified in the "sirens."

In view of this fourth stanza, one is tempted to observe that *it is no wonder* that the second fellow emerges from the abyss as a destroyed man and is described, in the fifth stanza as old, tired, broken, and drained. That the disenchantment is complete is made evident by a linguistic device as simple as it is ingenious. What was previously metaphoric, magical but merely suggestive imagery, is, at the end of the stanza, elucidated in sober and prosaic directness: "Und über die Wasser weht's kalt." For the first time, Eichendorff calls the element by its name and imperceptibly leads the reader on to the religious subject matter of the last stanza by means of the "Schifflein" (little ship), which is nothing more than the ancient topos of the ship of life.[3] It is also worth noting that it has now become still above the sucking, tugging whirlpool—but it is the stillness of death, of a downfall completed. ("Still" is often used by Eichendorff with this connotation, especially when combined with "cold," as is here the case; however, it can also have a positive meaning, that of a state of peacefulness or attainment of inner harmony. In poetry the context is always decisive.) The depiction of the two fates has been brought to an end and the last stanza contributes a summary, the "moral" of the poem:

> Es singen und klingen die Wellen
> Des Frühlings wohl über mir;
> Und seh' ich so kecke Gesellen,
> Die Tränen im Auge mir schwellen—
> Ach Gott, führ' uns liebreich zu Dir!

> The waves of spring are singing
> And ringing well over me,

And when I see such bold fellows
My eyes fill with tears—
O Lord, lead us gently to thee.

Once more the theme of spring with its familiar figurative
terms drawn from the spheres of music and water is sounded.
But this time the image is enriched by the highly revealing
preposition "über" (over). Man stands at the bottom of the
stream of life, and the elements of life relentlessly wash over
him. And now an "I," which was absent at the beginning, makes
its appearance in the third-to-last line. But it is not the lyrical "I"
of harmonic unity with the world; it stands for the average
person, or rather, for a concrete flesh-and-blood person, as opposed to the allegorical abstractions dealt with heretofore. For
what else are the "two fellows" if not figments of Eichendorff's
allegorizing imagination, embodiments of his ever-ready inclina-
tion to portray the typical and abstract in idealized figures.

Rather than treating intellectually the twin perils of withholding and giving oneself up (or "Sich verligen" and "Sich verliesen"[4] to use once more these expressions of medieval chivalry to
which Eichendorff felt so strongly bound), he lets them become
archetypal figures. The poem begins, innocently enough, with
the two fellows setting out together to meet with their personal
destinies. By a skillful and sparing selection of linguistic means,
however, they turn in Eichendorff's hands into human types who
have very little of a personal or individual character, who no
longer "are" but who "stand for." (The sirens of the fourth
stanza, too, are well on the way toward allegory, incorporating,
as they do, everything that belongs to spring, music, water, i.e.,
irresistible elementary forces.)

But what does the double allegory of losing and withholding
oneself signify for the concrete person, who now commences to
speak with the "I" of *tua res agitur?* There is no doubt that both
are to be avoided; that both, whether in a banal or tragic
manner, lead away from human predestination. The problems
of the poem are unequivocal, but no solution is furnished. Instead,
the last line is a deep sigh, a prayer to God for support in this
basic human dilemma. This very indecisiveness, however, this
obvious absence of any definitive decision, has been ingeniously
construed to correspond with the poem's message. For precisely

this not-knowing-which-way-to-turn is the prerequisite, indeed, the reverse side, of total, unconditional devotion, of placing one-self into God's hands, of a religious abandon. For this last line calls up the third and highest force in the triad of powers con-stituting the scope of Eichendorff's poetry: the bourgeois exist-ence with family, position, and regular earnings, to which Eichendorff, model Prussian civil servant, husband, and father, was bound with a goodly share of his life; the Romantic visionary realm, in which unity with nature, yearning for the world, the artistic existence, and eternal wandering were raised to meta-physical heights, and in which Eichendorff, as a poet by virtue of his imagination and intellect, had the most impressive share; and finally, the Catholic God of his childhood, in whom, accord-ing to the principle of *coincidentia oppositorum*, those two in-compatible ways meet and are reconciled.

I think that this poem sheds much light on Eichendorff's popu-larity. As a consummate work of art, it blends folkloric, narrative, and lyrical elements in an ingratiating fashion. Thanks to its rich allegory, it is easily understood and yet does not lack pro-fundity. Lending itself to song and engendering reflection as it does, it can satisfy the most disparate tastes.

To obtain an over-all impression of Eichendorff's poetic *idearium*, however, the outline obtained by our analysis of "Die zwei Gesellen" must be shaded in with particular features and contemporary colors from other poems. The previously men-tioned consistency of Eichendorff's lyrical world is helpful here. There is hardly another poet of consequence who managed with such a small number of basic poetic ideas and images. Inde-fatigably, the same landscape motives, the same color and sound values, and similar moods of feeling and atmosphere are repeated and slightly varied. As a result, not only does a dense, magical picture of the world arise even after brief reading, but some-thing that is, semantically, very curious, happens with the in-dividual words. Because they always recur, but each time in a different environment, in new contexts, in other rhythmic and tonal positions, and in varied rhyme combinations, an unusually rich aura of emotive associations and connotations gathers about the fixed core of meaning, making hunting for nuances into an unbelievably appealing game.

In "Die zwei Gesellen" the reader begins to sense that words such as "Frühling," "Haus," "Grund," "Stimmen," "farbig," "still," and "kalt" are endowed with a profusion of meaning and a property of mystery that cannot be comprehended merely from their use in everyday language, nor within the context of this one poem alone. What must be done is to acquire this vocabulary, to compile an Eichendorff dictionary, as it were, distilling the definitions from as many passages as possible. Basically, this procedure differs little from the path of perception one must take to any lyric-symbolistic poet. Only there is hardly another poetic language composed of so few words and, consequently, so easily acquired as is Eichendorff's. Therein, and in the concomitant wealth of feeling and fantasy lies the final, actual reason for the popularity of these poems and the love for their creator.

It cannot be the objective of this introduction to compile such an Eichendorff dictionary. But consideration of one other poem, picked from among many at random, will hopefully demonstrate the soundness of the method I have suggested.

No sooner do we read the first stanza of the poem "Frische Fahrt"[5] (Brisk Journey), which Eichendorff used as a kind of motto for his collected poems of 1815, than the characteristic "Eichendorff effect," a peculiar mixture of old and new impressions sets in:

> Laue Luft kommt blau geflossen,
> Frühling, Frühling soll es sein!
> Waldwärts Hörnerklang geschossen,
> Mut'ger Augen lichter Schein;
> Und das Wirren bunt und bunter
> Wird ein magisch wilder Fluss
> In die schöne Welt hinunter
> Lockt dich dieses Stromes Gruss.

> Tepid air comes flowing blue,
> Springtime, springtime's on its way!
> In the forest horns are sounding
> Bold eyes' luminous sheen;
> And the turmoil in its brilliance
> Becomes a magic wild stream,
> This beckoning river lures you down,
> Down into the beautiful world.

Immediately we find ourselves in familiar territory. It is the world of spring, the awakening of vegetative life, with which we were occupied in "Die zwei Gesellen." We recognize at once the liquid l-sounds of the two first lines as the allurement of life turned to sound; and, as in the former poem, here, too, the allurement is explicitly named. The jubilation, however, is no longer stated expressly. Instead, it is implicit in the exultant repetition of the key word "Frühling" (springtime). The metaphoric stream of life is present again, intensified in its synonym "river." Other traits appear in transmuted, but easily recognizable shape. Thus, for example, the "farbige" (colorful) world has become "bunt" (many-colored and animated); the lighting effect issuing from the "hellen Wellen" (bright waves) has been transferred to the "lichten Schein" (luminous sheen) of the bold eyes; the effect of depth created by the "Grund" (bottom) and the "Schlund" (abyss) as well as the fact that spring passed "over" the spectator is here achieved by the directional particle "hinunter" (down from here); whereas in place of the sirens the more general word "magisch" (magic) is used, unmistakably designating the same realm of witchcraft. There can be no doubt that this is the identical psychic landscape. And we add the missing second stanza:

> Und ich mag mich nicht bewahren!
> Weit von euch treibt mich der Wind,
> Auf dem Strome will ich fahren,
> Von dem Glanze selig blind!
> Tausend Stimmen lockend schlagen,
> Hoch Aurora flammend weht,
> Fahre zu! Ich mag nicht fragen,
> Wo die Fahrt zu Ende geht!

> And I will not preserve myself!
> The wind blows me far from you,
> On the stream I shall voyage,
> Blissfully blinded by the glow.
> A thousand voices ring alluring,
> High Aurora's flames are flaring,
> Onward! I will not question
> Where the journey is to end!

Here, too, we encounter well-known elements: the "thousand voices" and, once again, the allurement ("lockend"). The little boat is not expressly mentioned, but it is implicitly and indispensably present in the line "Auf dem Strome will ich fahren." What seems to be different is the stress. Whereas the reader had just been urgently warned against this voyage, it is here openly, indeed triumphantly, encouraged. This becomes evident from the fact alone that previously it had been one of the "Gesellen" who unmindfully headed his boat down into the stream of life, whereas here it is the "I" itself that yields to it, letting himself drift with the wind. (Nonetheless, the other position and the distance from it are still indicated by "weit von euch" in the second line.) And contrary to the former ideological objection, the decision seems here to be no less programmatically proclaimed: Und ich mag mich nicht bewahren!"

Still the assertion that the stress had changed was too categorical. For isn't it much more a matter of a different aspect, simply a phase within the same process? What aspects of this poem actually contradict the one considered earlier? The last statement reads, "Ich mag nicht fragen/Wo die Fahrt zu Ende geht!" Well, that isn't necessary, either. We know, after all, that it will inevitably end in shipwreck.[6] What we apparently have before us in the two stanzas of "Frische Fahrt" is a variation of the first and fourth stanzas of "Die zwei Gesellen," the remaining events portrayed there having been omitted. Instead, we have mere echoing associations, such as "bewahren" (preserving, shielding, withholding), which can only mean settling down to the solid, domestic ways of the third stanza in "Die zwei Gesellen," or the foreshadowing of destiny in the fifth stanza; for where else but in the abyss will the heedless voyager who "blindly" embarks upon his journey end! So it is the same idea, even though seen from a new point of view, which enlarges and emphasizes particular aspects of the same process predetermined from the very outset; it is a momentary experiment in which the poet savors a possibility to which he feels drawn while knowing only too well what speaks against it.

But at least as interesting as the detection of the connections of this poem with the earlier one are the deviations, or rather variations. Some of the elements in the picture of spring are new: the "Hörnerklang" (sound of horns) in the forest, the "Wirren" (turmoil, confusion) of the beautiful world, and the flaming "Aurora," the dawn transformed into a wild firebrand. (We have already seen that she can be, and is often evaluated differently in other contexts, even as divine and as the source of salvation.[7] This very conflict was the nourishment of Eichendorff's creativity.) A quick look about us teaches us that these things, too, are in no way unique or accidental, but that they crop up time and again in other poems. Positively or negatively tinged, "Wirren" appears in numerous derivatives (e.g., as "verworren" and "wirr"), and Aurora occurs in countless references and combinations. One could say that they have been spun into a web that envelops all of Eichendorff's lyrics.[8]

To round out these observations, we shall look at two other widely-known poems. The first of these will be contrasted with a no less famous poem by Goethe, in the hope of bringing to light poetic qualities in our author which are otherwise hidden. The second, one of Eichendorff's finest lyrical achievements, will hopefully reveal the fusion of formal elements with elements of content unique to him.

MIGNON

Johann Wolfgang Goethe

Kennst du das Land, wo die Zitronen blühn,
Im dunkeln Laub die Goldorangen glühn,
Ein sanfter Wind vom blauen Himmel weht,
Die Myrte still und hoch der Lorbeer steht,
Kennst du es wohl?
Dahin! Dahin
Möcht' ich mit dir, o mein Geliebter, ziehn!

Kennst du das Haus? auf Säulen ruht sein Dach,
Es glänzt der Saal, es schimmert das Gemach,
Und Marmorbilder stehn und sehn mich an:
Was hat man dir, du armes Kind, getan?
Kennst du es wohl?
Dahin! Dahin
Möcht ich mit dir, o mein Beschützer, ziehn!

Kennst du den Berg und seinen Wolkensteg?
Das Maultier sucht im Nebel seinen Weg,

in Höhlen wohnt der Drachen alte Brut,
Es stürzt der Fels und über ihn die Flut;
Kennst du ihn wohl?
Dahin! Dahin
Geht unser Weg; o Vater, lass uns ziehn![9]

Do you know the country where the lemon trees flower,
And the golden oranges glow in the dark foliage,
Where a gentle wind blows from the blue sky,
Where the myrtle stands quiet and the bay-tree towers up?
Do you know it perchance? That is where, oh, that is where
I would like to go with you, O my beloved!

You know the house? Its roof rests on pillars,
The hall gleams, the rooms glitter,
And marble statues stand and look at me:
"Poor child, what have they done to you?"
Do you know it perchance? That is where, oh, that is where
I would like to go with you, O my protector!

You know the mountain range and its cloudy path?
The mule seeks its way there in the mist,
The ancient brood of dragons dwells in caves,
The cliff falls sheer and the stream over it.
You know it perchance? That is where, oh that is where
Our way leads! O father, let us go![10]

SEHNSUCHT

Es schienen so golden die Sterne,
Am Fenster ich einsam stand
Und hörte aus weiter Ferne
Ein Posthorn im stillen Land.
Das Herz mir im Leib entbrennte,
Da hab' ich mir heimlich gedacht:
Ach, wer da mitreisen könnte
In der prächtigen Sommernacht!

Zwei junge Gesellen gingen
Vorüber am Bergeshang,
Ich hörte im Wandern sie singen
Die stille Gegend entlang:
Von schwindelnden Felsenschlüften,
Wo die Wälder rauschen so sacht,

Von Quellen, die von den Klüften
Sich stürzen in die Waldesnacht.

Sie sangen von Marmorbildern,
Von Gärten, die überm Gestein
In dämmernden Lauben verwildern,
Palästen im Mondenschein,
Wo die Mädchen am Fenster lauschen,
Wann der Lauten Klang erwacht
Und die Brunnen verschlafen rauschen
In der prächtigen Sommernacht.[11]

LONGING

So golden shone the stars,
I stood at the window, lonely,
And from afar I heard
A posthorn in the quiet land.
My heart burned in my breast,
And I mused to myself,
Oh, if I could travel along
In the splendid summer night.

Two young fellows went by
Past the mountain slope.
I heard them sing as they wandered
Through the quiet countryside:
Of dizzying rocky ravines
Where the forests softly rustle,
Of springs which from the cliffs
Plunge down into the wooded night.

They sang of marble statues
Of gardens spread over rocks
Growing wild in dusky arbors,
Of palaces lit by the moon
Where maidens listen at windows
For the echoing call of the lute,
And fountains sleepily murmur
In the splendid summer night.

If we chose to consider Eichendorff's "Sehnsucht," one of his
most enchanting and evocative poems, by itself, we would

stumble on something familiar in almost every line: the scenery of a bewitching night, the division between I and world, the two young fellows, the marble statues and the palaces, as well as the inevitable horns of the mail coach. A comparison with Mignon's song, however, should yield new perspectives.

For any such comparison between two poems to be fruitful, certain formal or thematic similarities are required. In this instance, they are plentiful. There is, first of all, the great common theme of longing. Eichendorff's poem even bears this title, and the famous poem by Goethe has long been considered the concentrated lyrical expression of the same feeling. In order to find this opinion justified, it is not even necessary to call to mind *Wilhelm Meisters Lehrjahre*, where the poem appears, or even to think of Mignon, the young heroine ravished by her longings, into whose mouth the poem is placed. In tone and image the lines themselves express a vast yearning for the faraway. But the correspondence does not end here, for the object of desire, too, is identical in both poems. Of course, in Goethe it is particularly distinct. The circumscription "Land, wo die Zitronen blühn" for Italy has become a platitude used by the most unpoetic minds. Eichendorff's cultivated landscape, evoked in the last stanza, with its marble statues and palaces, arbors, and lute must also be Italy. Once this has been established, another parallel immediately becomes apparent: not only do these poems have theme and object in common, but their construction as well. Both are divided into three parts, and in both each stanza is devoted to a particular stage of longing for Italy. In the first stanzas, the longing is postulated, while in the two following it appears concentrated in two separate phases.

But Eichendorff changed the sequence. Goethe portrays the distant goal in the second stanza, and the way toward it in the third. Eichendorff does the reverse, depicting first the movement towards the goal and only then the goal itself. Once this simple reversal has been accomplished, the identity is striking and extends even into details of the vocabulary. In both poems, the marble statues appear as well as the craggy mountains and the waters cascading over them. This kinship is too close to be mere coincidence; and one is tempted to consider Eichendorff's poem a variation on Goethe's, or even to assert that the younger poet, in publishing "Sehnsucht" in 1834, was presenting *his* version of Mignon's song. But this close connection is what is so intriguing; for there can be no doubt that, all surface resemblance notwithstanding, the poems are totally different. And even if the similarities could be ascribed to a certain playful intent on Eichendorff's part, the differences surely came about unconsciously and express the poetic temperaments which produced the two creations.

From the point of view of the historian of European literature, Goethe is classed as a Romantic, whereas the Germans, in particular at the time *Wilhelm Meister* was written, considered him to be the outstanding exponent of Classical poetry. With all due skepticism towards these overworked concepts, their contradiction does harbor a problem. A consideration of our two poems brings us closer to its solution. Seen by itself, Mignon's song is indeed full of Romantic features. The longing alone, the insatiable yearning of the Northerner for the southern landscape, the images of the rugged, almost foreboding Alpine pass with the allusion to the mythically primeval ("der Drachen alte Brut"), the evocation of the cultivated Italian landscape: all this is undoubtedly Romantic, if the expression is to have any meaning at all. Upon comparison with Eichendorff's poem, however, completely different traits come to the fore. One can see that our task is not an easy one. We have chosen in Mignon's song a most unsuitable object for demonstration of the Classical element in Goethe, but the results may be all the more convincing. Of course, the following must not be overlooked: Within the framework of *Wilhelm Meister*, the character of Mignon and everything connected with her represent a possibility that deviates from the general tendency of the novel, namely the Romantic possibility, which is ultimately rejected. Nonetheless, it represents a genuine experience on the part of Goethe.

One is immediately struck by the difference in the atmospheric quality. Mignon's is a song of daytime. The blue sky, the color effects, and the entire luminous impression make this obvious. Eichendorff's longing, on the other hand, is nocturnal. This could be felt even without the first line or the refrain-like evocation of the night so impressively culminating each stanza. The entire atmosphere and the tone itself are nocturnal. This is due primarily to the different sensory organs addressed by the two poems. The Goethe piece is almost totally based on visual perceptions. The

details stand out clearly and in sharp outline. The contrast of
the dark arbor with the golden oranges, the many colors, and
verbs like "glühn," "glänzen," "schimmern," "ansehen" allow no
other sensation to arise. Common longings and yearnings aside,
this is the vision of someone whose eyes are paramount in his
experiences. Eichendorff's images are acoustic. The horn is
"heard"; the young fellows announce their presence by "singing"
(in fact, their existence only becomes real when perceived
through the ears of the lyrical "I"); the forests and wells "rustle";
the lutes sound and the maidens listen. Indeed, the entire landscape, including the Italian one in the third stanza, is nothing
but an auditory reflex, which only becomes a picture by virtue
of the fellows' singing. The vagueness of the whole poem is
undoubtedly connected with this feature. Although details are
given, they have no independent existence. Instead, they are
indefinite and haphazardly listed phenomena which first take on
reality when joining together to form the overall atmospheric
impression. Small wonder, since they are only successively reported in the wanderer's song. Grammatically, this is accomplished by all the phenomena being prepositional objects: they
sing *about* dizzying ravines, *about* wells, *about* gardens, etc.
In Goethe's poem the matter is different. The objects stand "on
their own two feet." Every noun is connected with its own verb,
doing or being something on its own, and not simply a function
of hearing: the roof of the house *rests* on pillars, the mule *seeks*
his way, the myrtle, the laurel, and the marble statues *are
standing*.

The vagueness in Eichendorff results from other factors as well.
The gold of the stars in the first line is the only color to appear.
The other adjectives are either of an auditory nature, like the
"stille Land" (quiet land) or the "stille Gegend" (quiet countryside), or they are purposely obscure like the "dizzying" precipice,
the "dusky" arbors, or the inimitable and all-encompassing
"prächtig" (splendid, magnificent) describing the summer night.
It is also interesting that Goethe's momentary images ("es glänzt
der Saal, es stürzt der Fels," etc.) have evolved into processes in
Eichendorff. The fellows sing "as they wander through the countryside," and the gardens "grow wild."

Compared with Eichendorff, whose world, although of captivating beauty, seems completely chaotic, Mignon's song neces-

sarily imparts to the reader the impression of an almost logical and rational order. Each stanza could stand alone; grammatically, parataxis predominates; and the endings of sentences and lines usually coincide. In "Sehnsucht," the syntax and the grammatical forms are often strained ("Am Fenster ich einsam stand," "entbrennte"); and all in all, enjambment is prevalent. Goethe employs the refrain more emphatically than Eichendorff ("Kennst du" and "Dahin! Dahin!"). However, in contrast to "Sehnsucht," in which the succession "prächtige Sommernacht—Waldesnacht—prächtige Sommernacht" (splendid summer night—wooded night—splendid summer night) has a circular effect, the climactic sequence "Geliebter—Beschützer—Vater" has a logical or intentional quality about it.

In addition, perhaps the most significant details would be revealed by an analysis of sounds.[12] In view of the nature of our book, we shall refrain from such analysis and content ourselves, in conclusion, with observations of a more existentially determined difference. Even without the aid of the novel, no one can fail to detect the oppressed tone of heart in Goethe's poem. It is the very nature of longing, to be at once joy and torment. And yet this is not a voice in solitude, but a dialogue. It already starts with "you," and the partner is present to the end. The fulfillment of the dream of Italy is only considered conceivable together with the beloved, the guardian, the father—all designations which express a deep sense of finding shelter in the other individual. Indeed, the "I" does not appear at all until the refrain, the "you" absorbing it, along with its longing for Italy, so completely. It is a very different story with Eichendorff's "I." Not only does it appear three times in the nominative in the lyrical text, thus stressing its autistic character, but its loneliness is literally outspoken. Furthermore, the syntactical contortion of the second line, where in defiance of German usage the "lonely" has been stuck between subject and verb, brings about a provocative isolation of this "I." The window from which the world is perceived by it places itself between the two, as much a dividing as a connecting symbol. At the only spot where any sort of mutuality is at all implied—although a "you" is out of the question—it is immediately branded as an impossibility by the hypothetical subjunctive: "Ach, wer da mitreisen könnte" (Oh, if one could travel along). Here the loneliness, consuming in its might and precluding any exchange, has become a spoken presence!

Let us consolidate our findings: The musical-acoustic character of Eichendorff's poem, the chaotic nature of the perceptions, the nocturnal indistinctness of this world, the loneliness and exclusion of the subject whose experiences these are, and the dynamic character of the processes are a singularly pure expression of the Romantic inner turmoil. By comparison, an eminently Romantic poem like Goethe's "Mignon," all similarity of image and theme notwithstanding, seems like the prototype of Classical order, clarity, and rationality.

At the end of the chapter, let us cast one look at the poem "Mondnacht"[13] (Moon Night), which was so delightfully set to music by Robert Schumann. It is generally classed with Eichendorff's sacred poetry, but basically it has no more religious ingredients than most of his nature poems.

Es war, als hätt' der Himmel
Die Erde still geküsst,
Dass sie im Blütenschimmer
Von ihm nun träumen müsst'.

Die Luft ging durch die Felder
Die Ähren wogten sacht,
Es rauschten leis die Wälder,
So sternklar war die Nacht.

Und meine Seele spannte
Weit ihre Flügel aus,
Flog durch die stillen Lande,
Als flöge sie nach Haus.

It was as if the heaven
Had gently kissed the earth,
And now in blossoms' shimmer
She had to dream of him.

The air went through the fields,
Smoothly waving grain,
And softly rustling woods,
So star-clear was the night.

And my soul spread
Wide its wings,
Flew through the quiet lands
As if for home.

Here we are almost exclusively dealing with pure sound. Even
someone without command of German would be moved by this
rhythmic and symphonic intensity. The progression of the vowel
rows in the four first lines, *a ä i, e i ü, i ü i, i äu ü,* has something
captivating about it that cannot be specified. And so it goes
with all the stanzas. The poem is all of one casting. In addition,
it has such an overwhelming simplicity of expression that one
could call it cunningly constructed if it weren't so unintentional
and completely unpretentious. "Die Luft ging durch die Felder":
can there be anything simpler than that? But even this inconspicuous little sentence is artfully constructed. The verb of motion "went" is somehow so childish and so primitive that immediately the idea of magic in nature as conceived by childish
individuals or primitive peoples comes to the fore.

On the level of meaning, this "going" transforms the air into a
divine messenger who establishes a connection between heaven
and earth. This, in turn, beautifully fits the air of creaturely piety
breathed by the entire poem. Of course, this only becomes clear
when seen together with other details that are similarly employed. The rhyme "Himmel-Schimmer" also has this childish-
primitive quality. Actually it is no real rhyme and, singled out,
seems the product of a childish soul so stirred by religious feeling that he has failed to find the rhyming words. Now we notice
that whenever is the relationship between above and below,
heaven and earth referred to, a similar slight discrepancy appears (cf. the rhyme in the last stanza "spannte-Lande," which
will be further discussed) to signify that the correspondence
can never be complete. I do not claim that Eichendorff consciously planned this effect. But the share which rationality,
the poet's "artistic know-how," had in forming an object of art is
not definable. It is only certain that those effects that are affixed
like flourishes or ornaments are esthetically fatal, because dis-
cerned intention tends to cool the observer's enthusiasm. If
idiosyncrasies of language support the pervasive character of

a work of art, as is here the case, they belong to its structure and probing their "intentionality" becomes inessential.

In "Mondnacht" we again come across Eichendorff's favorite images and expressions. "Still," "sacht," "leis" (still, gently, softly) are such examples; and a line like "Es rauschten leis die Wälder" (softly rustled the woods) bears his inimitable hallmark. But it appears as if it were purged of all superfluities and immersed in a simplicity that is no longer of this earth. Again we are dealing with a nocturnal poem, but here, for once, it is a night free of any torment. The longing is still present, the allurement of spring can still be felt, but only as an aroma, a soft movement that has no compelling drive about it.

How unlikely that something approaching a cosmology is concealed behind this pure simplicity, and yet this is the case. One is almost tempted to ignore the meaning of the words and just absorb the sound. But the stanzas contain a message. Nature's capacity to enchant is not just presented as a fact but as resulting from a mythological cause. The divine origin is reverently cloaked in impenetrability by the use of the subjunctive construction of the first line, thus presented as the object of faith. It signifies that we cannot assert it with certainty; but it seems that the unspeakable fascination emanating from even the simplest of phenomena in nature is of divine origin, and man's love for them is nothing but the reflection of this erotic, procreating union, most delicately expressed in the verb "geküsst" (kissed). The second stanza details these phenomena: night, summer, springtime—the "Wogen der Ähren" (smoothly waving grain) being an attribute of summer, the "Blütenschimmer" (blossoms' shimmer) one of spring. They are not just grouped together in the passage but, as in the first pages of *Taugenichts*, occur together. This serves to reinforce the mythical character of the seasons. Spring is not a *phase* but a *potency* of the earth.

As in the Bible, this procreation progresses in hierarchic steps, rising from the tellurian phenomena to the height of creation, the human being. The cosmic kiss of heaven impels man, or rather his esoteric side, to wander. In the last stanza, the circle of creation is completed. The beauty of earth culminates in the human soul, which lifts itself in flight to heaven. How movingly its return to the heavenly homeland is conveyed, again finding expression in the conjectural subjunctive and the imperfect rhyme. Simultaneously, however, the hard-sounding "spannte" finds its mild and hope-bearing resolution in the softness of the assonance "Lande."

In this unsurpassable composition, Eichendorff's quiet lyrical poetry, its inseparable blend of simplicity and refinement, celebrates its mythical climax.

CHAPTER 4

The Novellas

MUCH of what has been said about Eichendorff's novels will necessarily hold true of the shorter tales he wrote (and, by the same token, the latter may shed light on obscure elements in the full-length narratives). The peculiarities of a prose writer, particularly if he is a craftsman with the strong idiosyncratic propensities of Eichendorff, will assert themselves in whatever medium he chooses to express himself. What precisely is a novella? Skepticism seems to be in order with regard to the orthodox view that recognizes it as a clearly defined genre. In German literary theory in particular, the novella has been accorded extensive treatment, many learned volumes having been devoted to the task of coming to grips with the form. But it is precisely this need for ever better, ever different theories, this obvious dissatisfaction of every new author with the findings of his predecessors, and—to use an understatement—the resulting lack of unanimity, that occasion a few irreverent questions, such as: Is there such a thing as a "novella"? Is it different from a short novel? And if so, is it possible to describe the genre in terms that will encompass a significant number of stories and at the same time provide reliable standards for excluding others that do not meet specific requirements?

It is easier to side with those scholars, increasing in number, who see in the novella merely a medium-length narrative.[1] It is not difficult to concede that there exist loosely constructed stories which, charming as they may be, reflect the style of the great raconteur. And conversely it cannot be denied that these can be contrasted with the skillfully composed tales, painstakingly controlled in every detail, tending toward symbolism and concerned with serious intellectual problems. It has been suggested that the latter should be called "novellas." But there is no great advantage in doing so since, in practice, it will be extremely difficult to distinguish between the two. They will have innumerable features in common, not the least important of which is a certain limitation in length, somewhere between the average short story and the average full-length novel. The duration of his tale is a strongly determining factor for the author, and a medium-length narrative will partly deprive him of, and partly supply him with, certain opportunities inherent in or absent from stories of a different length. Beyond the obvious differences in talent, background, and orientation, the limitations of length will dispose the writers to employing similar literary devices. For this reason, whenever the term "novella" is used in the following pages, it is to be understood as a synonym of short tale or medium-length story with no other specific implications.

Now that the question of genre, which was bound to arise in connection with Eichendorff's novellas, has been touched upon, a number of the poet's most significant novellas will be analyzed as separate works of art, with the attention focused on a few main traits in each. Even a cursory glance across the panorama of his shorter tales tends to justify this approach. They are significantly different from one another. Picaresque tales, allegories, literary satires, stories of adventure, historical novellas, and narratives made up of a mixture of these types are represented in Eichendorff's oeuvre.

I Viel Lärmen um nichts

Much Ado about Nothing is a self-parody where the treatment is so light that questions of plot, ideology, and poetical doctrine can safely be relegated to a distant background. What remains is pure form, i.e., Eichendorff's quintessence as a story-teller; and the lessons to be learned from it about Eichendorff's style may justify starting our discussion with this relatively late product (1832), by far not his best, but certainly one of his most revealing stories. One gets the impression that Eichendorff intended to spread out once more before the eyes of his readers the great wealth of his imagination, without recourse to a meticulously preplanned order, but rather in the manner of a merchant in an oriental bazaar who proudly piles up his magnificent wares. Literary satire and moon-lit forests, haunted castles and opulent country estates, disguises and mistaken identities, allegorical riddles and dream visions, feasts and parties, hunting expeditions and society weddings, thunderstorms and sunrises, solitary foot journeys and pointless outings on horseback: such are the elements of Eichendorff's romantic fairy-tale world (even the French horns are not lacking and, at the end, the obligatory honeymoon trip to Italy is enacted!).

The figures who populate it are also quite familiar by now, even though they rarely appear in this abundance and variety. There are the counts and the princes, the countesses and their chambermaids, ladies of high society and millers' daughters close to nature, allegorical characters, marble statues come-to-life and sleeping servants, derelict guardians of the unconscious. There are the ghostly castellans, poets and lesser literati, genuine hunters and false hunters' assistants who, in fact, are baronesses in disguise. And as if this were not enough, Eichendorff reintroduces into *Viel Lärmen um nichts* a number of characters from earlier works. They are greeted with a surprise paralleling our own: "For heaven's sake! Count Leontin from *Ahnung und Gegenwart!*"[2]

In view of such profusion and playful arbitrariness, it is not surprising that Eichendorff has failed to imprint an order on this chaos that would make a well-wrought work of art out of this figment of a fertile imagination. Indeed, it is questionable whether he actually intended to achieve this goal in the case of *Much Ado about Nothing.* From the title bristling with self-sarcasm to the tale's conclusion when the lovers, finally united, once again go to Italy while the poet Eichendorff, having entered the world of his own fiction, stays behind to record their story, many indications suggest that more is at stake than mere romantic irony. Eichendorff was a more conscious and careful craftsman than the surface of his narratives would lead one to expect. The improbable accumulation of confusing motives, incongruous figures, and crazy snatches of action, the presence of characters such as Leontin, Julie, and Faber from *Ahnung und Gegenwart,* the poet's personal intervention in the plot, the allegorical figure of Mr. Public, the frequently unmotivated episodes, and the clichés and exaggerations indicate that the writer intended to present in this novella, whatever else he wished to signify, a parody of his own narrative style. Whatever the truth of this observation, it stands to reason that the visible seams of a costume which was made rapidly for mere entertainment can reveal as much, or even more, about the working methods of the tailor than a carefully sewn garment. Similarly, a light poetic work, improvised on a sudden impulse, is capable of providing as much information about the working secrets of an entire workshop as a serious and ambitious work of craftsmanship. Let us use *Much Ado about Nothing* for the purpose of concentrating on one technical feature of the story, its ending, and try to learn from it as much as possible about Eichendorff's narrative craft.

The conclusion of *Much Ado* is remarkable insofar as the "true" poet (der rechte Dichter)—in this case one probably does not commit a grave sin against subtlety by simply identifying him with Eichendorff himself—is assigned the task of recording the events just as they have actually occurred. "Countess Aurora," the reader is informed in the very last lines,

told me everything as it took place, from beginning to end. And I am sitting in the magnificent garden, high in spirit, with a plate full of fresh peaches next to me into which she had sunken her white little teeth as a souvenir for me, the morning air is merrily leafing through the papers spread out before me; not far away, red deer are grazing in a shadowy dale, and, as I am writing these lines, Aurora and Willibald are just passing through the glistening landscape far below, on their way to Italy. I can still hear them singing in the distance

> And over the rocky ramparts
> And across the green plain
> There is endless and joyous confusion,
> Now our foot trip can finally start![3]

It is possible to demonstrate that almost every phrase and expression in these concluding sentences carries unusual weight. Eichendorff's tales are riddles in which free rein seems to be given to every madness. That the crazy skein should be unraveled in the end, and that there should come a final enlightenment, is no more than the readers feel entitled to expect. But if one stops to consider *how* this is done, by what means of narration the ultimate reckoning is accomplished, one is nevertheless amazed. What is achieved by the introduction of a poet into his own

narrative from the point of view of Romantic irony—a shattering
of illusions and liberation of the artistic spirit—has been said
often enough with sufficient clarity. We are here concerned with
one further effect of the device, and that is the reduction of
distance between the world of the reader and that of the poetic
events. The result is a kind of guarantee for their authenticity.
When the poet himself intervenes as an actor in the affairs of
the plot for the purpose of putting them in order, as Eichendorff
does at the end of *Much Ado,* the action is shifted, as it were, to
another plane of reality, closer to that of the reader.

In the case of *Much Ado,* even more special significance is
attached to Eichendorff's personal appearance in the story. At
the time when he, the "true poet," enters the narrative stage, the
events of the plot have already been brought to a preliminary
conclusion. The talented but dissolute Romano (observe the
names; for their treatment is the same as in *Ahnung und Gegenwart* and, for that matter, everywhere else in Eichendorff's prose
work) has left the scene without reaching a satisfactory solution
of his existential problems; there is none for the incorrigible
egotist. As a result, no obstacle to the union of Mr. Public and
Countess Aurora seems to remain. Triumphantly they betake
themselves to the groom's country mansion, in order to celebrate
their wedding. They are accompanied by the "false poets," called
"novelists" (writers of novellas, to be precise), in whose limited
imagination from the very beginning this betrothal had loomed
large as the only possibility. They are now eagerly intent upon
"finishing their novella with an elaborate wedding."[4] The professional interest and the unending comments with which these
gentlemen have been following the events, as well as the peculiar
turn that they finally take, suggest that in *Much Ado about
Nothing* "something" is at stake after all, namely the fashioning
of a novella from life, or rather the proper relationship between
life and art. It is this question, and of course the mockery with
which Eichendorff treats the novelists, that have led to the not
entirely satisfying designation of this work as one of the poet's
"literary satires."

As soon as the plot is recapitulated in the manner in which we
have attempted to do so, one realizes immediately that much
about it is disquieting and, what is worse, that many a riddle
remains without solution. Is it really acceptable to the reader

that the superficial Public should be rewarded for his silliness with the hand of the fabulous countess, a second Diana and almost "Holy Poetry Personified"? And what about Aurora herself? Is there not something contradictory about her that escapes reconciliation? How are certain strangely suspect habits and attributes of hers compatible with such a lofty mission? Moreover, what is to become of Willibald, a friend and young replica of the poet himself? His encounter with the beautiful stranger in the forest certainly demands a happy continuation. And what is the secret surrounding the mysteriously "delicate hunter's boy" Florentin, in whose manner and being so many girlish traits could be detected? (We are deliberately omitting several lesser motives which also require explanation.)

One effect attributable to the appearance of the poet Eichendorff in the novella is that things begin to clear up as soon as he steps in. Florentin turns out to be, as we have long suspected, the real Countess Aurora. The alleged countess, whom the unsuspecting Public is about to marry, is none other than her clever but vulgar chambermaid. Simultaneously, Willibald finds and recognizes his lost beloved, whereupon the union is rapidly consummated and the couple's Italian journey decided upon.

From this point of view, we may observe an effect similar to one already registered: a gradual uncovering of successive levels of reality is taking place, and the poet has skillfully substituted a deeper or fuller conception of reality for a lesser one. The commonplace literati are satisfied with a run-of-the-mill or humdrum solution of the conflicts, and they hasten to commit to paper their shallow and distorted story, unworried by Leontin's spontaneous warning prompted by nothing but his love of truth: "Are you . . . crazy? You have been pitifully deceived."[5] The whole truth is revealed only to the penetrating gaze of the true poet. The wisdom of the "novelists" comprises but a misunderstood fragment of life.

Thus one might regard the quest for a "heightened sense of reality" as the center of the novella's dynamics. What remains to be seen now is by what narrative technique this effect is achieved. The expression "enlightenment" was used to describe the condition of inner clarity resulting from the heightened reality attained at the conclusion of the novella. In fact, this term is also applicable to the effect of a natural phenomenon Eichen-

dorff describes as an "objective correlative" in the closing pages
of his work. That a writer should use natural events as an ac-
companiment or counterpoint to the human destinies running
their course in the foreground, is in no way uncommon.

Sunrises are so frequent in the works of Eichendorff that they
constitute something like the author's signature. The fact, however, that the last impression left by so many of his prose narratives is the brightness caused by the rising sun requires close
analysis. "Die Sonne ging eben prächtig auf" (the sun was just
rising majestically),[6] for example, are the closing words of his
epic masterpiece *Ahnung und Gegenwart.* But this is certainly
no exception. On the contrary, it is the same wherever one
looks. "Alle schwiegen, die Sonne ging soeben auf vor ihnen und
warf ihre funkelnden Lichter über die Erde" (They were all
silent, the sun was just rising in front of them and threw its
sparkling light across the earth);[7] "Da ging die Sonne prächtig
auf" (At that moment the sun rose magnificently);[8] Und als die
Sonne aufging, flog das Schiff schon übers blaue Meer" (And
as the sun rose, the ship was already racing across the blue sea);[9]
"Die Sonne schien schon hell ins Zimmer" (The sun already
shone brightly into the room)[10]—these are merely a few of the
almost rigid formulae by which Eichendorff manages to immerse
the endings of his stories in the brilliant radiance of early morning. To call this a subjective or emotive use of nature, as has
been so often done, is a grave mistake. We are now in a position
to understand the very precise theological meaning of this (and
similar) atmospheric effects that were all too readily dismissed
as romantic clichés.

Again at the end of *Much Ado,* but this time under masterful
control, the same phenomenon is depicted in a long, drawn-out
sequence. From the appearance of the poet to the concluding
paragraph quoted above, the clarification of the true state of
affairs proceeds on more than five printed pages, and in artful
correspondence to this spiritual enlightenment, references to the
gradually paling night and the triumphant rise of the sun are
interwoven. Taken out of their context and strung together, they
result in the following images of nature. At first, we are reminded that night still reigns supreme[11] and that "Wälder,
Wiesen and Dörfer flogen . . . im hellen Mondschein vorüber"
(forests, meadows, and villages flew past in the bright moon-

light).[12] But "die Sterne fingen schon an zu verlöschen" (the stars already began to dim)[13] and soon thereafter "die durch rotseidene Gardinen brechende Dämmerung" (dawn filtering through red-silken curtains)[14] arrives. "Eine duftige Kühle quoll . . . plötzlich erfrischend" (a fragrant coolness suddenly streamed in)[15] from the garden. "Jenseits ging soeben der Mond hinter den dunklen Bergen unter, von der anderen Seite flog schon eine leise Röte über den ganzen Himmel, die geheimnisvolle Gegend aber lag unten wunderbar bleich in der Dämmerung, nur im Tale fern blitzte zuweilen schon ein Strom auf" (Beyond, the moon was just setting behind the dark mountains, from the other side a delicate red was already flashing across the entire sky, but the mysterious region lay wondrously pale down below in the twilight, and only in the distant valley did a river sparkle up from time to time).[16] "Einzelne Schlaglichter fielen schon durch die Wipfel" (occasional shafts of light already shot through the tree crowns).[17] And finally, when the long-awaited lover steps forth after all and is recognized by the poet as his boyhood friend Willibald, we read: "Hinter den fernen, blauen Bergen aber ging soeben die Sonne auf und blitzte so morgenfrisch über die ganze Landschaft" (But the sun was rising behind the distant blue mountains and sent flashes fresh as the morning across the entire landscape).

The "Morgenluft" and the "glänzende Landschaft" of the last lines are merely a final reflection, a recapitulation brought in by the poet in order to confirm once more the recaptured brightness. All this has been woven, imperceptibly and little by little, into the action as it rises toward its final solution; an unobtrusive side effect, and yet more than mere background music or an attempt to integrate an act of nature with a state of the mind—an integration in which Eichendorff always excels. Is this Aurora, pursued by every character in the plot—the Public, the dime-a-dozen poets, the supreme egotist as well as the true poetic youth in whom nature and the spirit have combined to the perfection which is poetry—is this Aurora still only human?

Familiar now with the little game he likes to play with names, and cognizant of the metaphysical character of this sunrise, which signifies no less than a supernatural illumination of our terrestrial troubles, we are forced to see in this Aurora, as it were, the mystical union of a human and a divine phenomenon.

The play on the word Aurora, on the one hand designating a natural phenomenon, and on the other being both a woman's and a goddess' name, occurs repeatedly in Eichendorff's prose writings. In support of the above interpretation, one can point to the novel *Dichter und ihre Gesellen,* where the identification of the central heroine with Aurora is beyond any doubt, for the simple reason that the girl's real name is Fiammetta. "Now I am truly Aurora"[18] she says plainly and categorically at one point.

This is reminiscent of certain gestures in the masterworks of world literature where a material phenomenon or object can symbolize a mental state or a turn in a human destiny. Just as the purely physical rise of the *deus ex machina,* after he has disentangled the human confusions in an ancient tragedy, was supposed to be paralleled by a moral uplift in the audience; or as the spectators' knowledge of a conciliatory turn in history was calculated to shed a mitigating light upon some of Schiller's historical dramas (for example *Don Carlos* and *Mary Stuart,* where the liberation of the Netherlands and the later accession of the Stuarts to the British throne, respectively, are to justify the central characters), so Eichendorff, too, dispels the clouds of human inadequacy by means of his sublime sunrises. A counterpart to these, and indeed their logical supplement, are the many evening moods and sunsets with which the majority of his prose works begin, for example *Dichter und ihre Gesellen,*[19] *Das Marmorbild,*[20] *Die Entführung,*[21] *Die Glücksritter,*[22] as well as the novella under consideration.[23] (The most notable exception is *Ahnung und Gegenwart,* where the sun has just risen as the novel opens.)

We are now ready to draw our conclusions. Among the favorite stems in Eichendorff's vocabulary is "wirr" (confused) with all of its derivatives and cognates, including the unusual and somewhat vague intransitive verb "wirren" (which cannot be adequately rendered in English) as well as the adjective "verworren" (confused), for which the young Goethe also had an understandable predilection. These words appear everywhere in Eichendorff's prose and poetry. Their abundance is symptomatic of his confused plots. In *Much Ado,* the most introspective of his tales, the author perceptively puts the following words into the mouth of Willibald: "Es war mir, als sei ich in ein wahnsinniges Märchen verstrickt" (It was as if I were implicated in a crazy fairy tale).[24] However, these confusions are not the result of a mad uncontrolled imagination but a conscious attempt on the part of the writer to reflect life on earth and the condition of the human soul. There is no doubt what he meant by the motto from Shakespeare's *A Midsummer Night's Dream* which precedes the novella:

> If we shadows have offended,
> Think but this, and all is mended,
> That you have but slumber'd here
> While these visions did appear.
> And this weak and idle theme
> No more yielding but a dream . . .

The German version of these lines, which Eichendorff uses, is even more to the point of his intention: "Wenn wir Schatten euch beleidigt,/ O so glaubt—und wohl verteidigt/ Sind wir dann—, ihr alle schier/ Habet nur geschlummert hier/ Und geschaut in Nachtgesichten/ Eures eignen Hirnes Dichten."[25] In this translation the last line identifies the "visions" as figments of the subject's own imagination.

And yet, of course, the sunlight at the end is not "realism" in the banal sense that nightmare, inconsequential in the last analysis, is shaken off as the day breaks, in whose light everything will be easier to bear. For the symbolism of confusion and clarity does not suggest the removal of a fanciful phantasmagoria by empirical reality, but a life in puzzlement and anxiety which finds its fulfillment through a belief in higher truth, a transition from suffering in life to an acceptance of life in the hope for divine grace. The deer have lost their fear of man—this is an almost chiliastic image—the wind playfully ruffles his paper, and then, in a final return of daring boisterousness, a last mention is made of "Wirren," of continued wanderings. This is possible because, even though life goes on, nothing untoward can happen anymore.

It must be pointed out that the great majority of Eichendorff's prose works, long or short, end in this becalmed manner. And it is touching to observe how the human self, having gone through the hell and paradise of terrestrial allurements and having been shaken by the paroxysm of their feverish pursuits—and be they nothing worse than the terrors of a literary satire—is allowed to rest in bed,[26] cracking almonds in tender company,[27] or facing a dish of nibbled peaches. The promise is not of rest in a more solidly empirical reality than the one just gone through but in one which is safe, religiously hale, and guaranteed by divine protection. This is what is really behind the flirtatious domestic game with almonds in *Taugenichts* and peaches in *Much Ado.* The bite marks, stemming from the little teeth of the mythical Aurora, are visible tokens sanctifying the earthly and, alas, so perishable fruits. In retrospect from this ultimate insight, that which has been gone through, life without transcendence, can be interpreted as a "dream," a "fata morgana,"[28] or as a "crazy fairy tale."[29]

Hell and paradise: this ambiguity pervading life on earth must be understood. The night, dark and yet moonlit, is ambivalent in Eichendorff's cosmos, as we have already had occasion to see. Only when the sun is rising do the fuzzy outlines become firm and unequivocal. Why should the poet not abandon himself to the carefree gaiety which itself cannot but be of divine origin. The world lies before him transfigured. Night's magic twilight, beautiful and tormenting at the same time—as anything magic would be—has been replaced by a soothing clarity. The riddles have been solved, the unknown comprehended, the mysteries explained, and the confused relationships disentangled. The divine light of grace has been poured out over the whole of creation. And so the relieved poet can exclaim: "Es war ja alles wieder sein" (Everything, everything was again his);[30] "es ist mir, als würde noch alles gut werden" (I have a feeling as if everything were still to turn out well);[31] or even "es war alles, alles gut!" (all, all was well!).[32] This deep rejoicing at the end of many of Eichendorff's prose works, whether explicitly stated or implicit in the closing cadences, must not be mistaken for sentimental optimism. Its true poetic meaning can only be understood by also perceiving the metaphysical peril conveyed through the allegory. And this act of understanding will, at the same time, succeed in establishing the difference between symbolic novellas with tragic overtones and Biedermeier idylls, with which some of Eichendorff's stories have been erroneously compared.

II Das Marmorbild

We have repeatedly observed Eichendorff's penchant for allegory. In his story *Das Marmorbild (The Marble Statue)* of

1819, he develops the allegorical style to a peak of perfection, thus deepening our understanding of his private mythology. We shall pursue two questions in our survey of this novella: how it is "made" and what the philosophy expressed in it actually connotes.

From the very beginning, *The Marble Statue* deals with the experiences of a young man in the city of Lucca, Florio, who is distinguished by his unquenchable yearning for self-fulfillment and a certain, as yet unripe, poetic talent. Florio is one of those "poetic souls" whom Eichendorff deems alone worthy of being taken seriously and destined to become complete human beings. What he encounters in Lucca is so fraught with significance that every detail—indeed almost every word—holds promise of a deeper meaning, which the reader is anxious to unearth. And the words with which the author describes a ball could be placed as motto over the entire fairy-tale narrative: "Many were masked, and unwittingly their peculiar appearance often lent the charming game a sudden, deep, and almost terrifying significance."[33]

The author has built into his portrayals many unmistakable "signals" in order to alert the reader to the allegorical nature of the account. Perhaps one of the most distinct of these is the expression "dark powers"[34] with which, at the end of the novella, where, as is almost always the case in Eichendorff's writings, mysteries are resolved (in concert with the various stages of a sunrise), he designates the erotic seduction threatening Florio. The seductive figures, the "dark powers," are also easily recognized as being allegorical. Of all of these figures, the goddess Venus is the most obvious. Driven by irresistible desire, Florio leaves his lodging on his first night in Lucca. At the edge of a pond, he comes across a statue of Venus and is enraptured by its beauty. Eichendorff sees to it that in the course of the narration, one recognizes in the woman who enthralls his senses and his entire being, the marble figure come to life. "They were," the reader is informed at their first meeting, "without doubt the features, the entire figure of the beautiful Venus statue he had seen that night at the pond."[35] A cosmic dimension is then added by expanding the allegory into a vital force: "He felt incredibly well. The beautiful marble statue had come to life and descended from its pedestal, the quiet pond was suddenly transformed into a vast landscape, the stars therein into flowers, and the entire spring

into the image of the lovely one."[36] This identity is gradually
substantiated by hundreds of sensory impressions—such as the
classic style of her house, the luxuriant fertility of the garden—
as well as by allusions in songs and conversations, until it gains
an aura of life. We shall return for a closer look at some of these
devices.

Venus is aided in the business of snaring souls by the knight
Donati, her "relative,"[37] who is assigned the role of go-between.
Since it is apparent that in this thoroughly allegorized story all
names have a meaning related to the total scheme—hence Florio,
a budding youth not yet defined and courted by all, or Fortunato,
the joyful, luck-bringing minstrel—it has often been attempted
to interpret the more difficult and obscure name of Donati allegorically. One possibility would be to link it with that of Alesso
di Guido Donati, the fourteenth-century Tuscan poet whose
"songs were often filled with undisguised sensuality."[38] Another
plausible suggestion is to take the name as an Italianized form of
the Greek god of death, Thanatos; for in spite of the knight's
appeal, his "deep eye sockets,"[39] his handsome but pale and dissolute face, his pale lips, and his death-like sleep are sinister
traits.[40] This conjecture is supported by a philosophical song
sung by Fortunato just prior to Donati's first appearance, in
which Venus is connected with the death god.[41] Be that as it
may, the close inner relationship between these "dark powers,"
definitely existent on the plot level, is made manifest by the
use of color symbolism and placed in a mythological nexus.

At Donati's first entrance (which meets with the stunned
silence of the spectators, since at the beginning of the story
Fortunato had described in his thematic song the "most silent
of all the guests" who was "garlanded with blossoming pop-
pies"),[42] the knight's jewels are said to emit "golden green rays,"[43]
while the Venus figure is wearing on her bosom a gem which
cast "long, golden green rays over the meadow in the evening
sun."[44] And at the moment of Florio's disenchantment, the entire
spooky complex enters the realm of Christian mythology, again
with the same color symbolism: "Hardly had he fervently spoken
the words ["Lord, do not let me get lost in the world"], when
he noticed on the windowsill grass and clumps of weeds such as
grow on old ruins. A hissing snake darted out and coiling its
golden green tail, plunged into the abyss below."[45]

Throughout the novella, the dark powers are contrasted with light powers. In an almost choreographically exact allegorical parallel, they are each represented by a female and a male figure, who also contend for Florio's soul. Donati is a black, nocturnal shadow, while Fortunato seems to be identified with the morning. The knight is somber and deathlike and, on rare occasions, animated by a fierce fury, while the poet is high-spirited, gleeful, and adverse to all melancholy, but nonetheless adamant and quickly roused in matters concerning his charge, Florio. The two are diametrically opposed in another respect as well: their relation to Christianity. Like the devil's steed in the fairy tale, Donati's horse shies on entering the Christian city of Lucca (and with a wild curse that betrays the gentleness he otherwise assumes, Donati thereupon drops his plan to accompany the youth to his quarters),[46] and like the evil figure in the *Märchen,* he tries to entice Florio to join a Sunday hunting party. His proposal is not well received. "Hunting," the piously reared Christian youth indignantly replies, "today, on the holy day?" Again the author uses the critical moment to lift the mask of Donati's proper and virtuous bearing and let his true nature shine through menacingly. "'Now, really,' the knight interrupts him, laughing spitefully and horribly, 'do not tell me that you want to go to church, linking arms with your sweetheart, kneeling on the footstool and devoutly muttering gesundheit! when your neighbor sneezes!'"[47]

But typical of the hero of fairy tales or legends, Florio exhibits towards this mockery the naive steadfastness which will ultimately let him triumph over all temptations. "I do not know what you mean," Eichendorff has him innocently reply, "and you may go on laughing at me, but I could not hunt today. Out there all work has come to rest, and forests and fields seem adorned in God's honor, as if angels were passing over them through the heavenly blue—so still, so peaceful and merciful it is at this time!"[48] And immediately the evil one is vanquished, just as the slightest reference to Christianity disarms him and his helper, Venus. "Donati stood at the window sunk in thought, and Florio thought that he had seen him secretly shudder as he gazed out at the Sunday stillness of the fields."[49] Florio's fear that he has danced "too long" at the masked ball also reminds one of a fairy tale. However, this resemblance is superficial, a "blind motif," as it were, which creates the aura of a fairy tale but does not take over its techniques or problems. (This is clearly illustrated by the central motif of coming to life which the story shares with the fairy tale, using it, however, for quite different purposes.) This encounter should have sufficed to enable Florio to see through his acquaintance; but this insight is still to come. We have dealt at such length with their exchange to show the means employed by Eichendorff to depersonalize his figures, and, by purposely ignoring psychologically credible behavior, to make them into bearers of an idea. The presence of many such passages is what compels us to speak of allegory and to seek allegorical significance even where it is not immediately discernible.

Much is added to the general allegorical impression by Fortunato's contrasting attitude. He never tires of warning against the heathen magic—from his "Take heed!" at the beginning of the story to the "old, pious song" he sings in the garden at the moment of the most dangerous temptation, giving Florio the strength to think of the Christian God and resist the heathen goddess. Incidentally, the words "magic mountain,"[50] which precede his warning, are the first direct allusion to Venus, and the mysterious minstrel who attracts youth has the double meaning of spring—i.e., spring subject to regeneration and petrification, to life and death—and of Donati, which shows how tightly the web of allegory is woven. (The danger Fortunato warns against is more complex than has yet been expressed: he not only deprecates nature worship but also ardent devotion to nighttime, hence the Romantic and autistic poetic life.)

The contrast intended with these two figures is most clearly expressed by an image which instantly illuminates their relationship to Florio. At the outset of the novel, right after the two opposing actors have been introduced, they accompany the youth to the city where he is to find quarters. This simple situation is described with the following suggestive sentences:

All three mounted . . . their horses and headed together towards the nearby town. Fortunato did not utter a word on the way. Donati, all the friendlier, poured forth his delicate, well-turned phrases; Florio, joy still echoing in him, rode silently between the two like a dreamy maiden.[51]

The silence of the one, the loquaciousness and false courtliness of the other indicate their contrary goals. The simile, temporarily treating Florio as a girl, emphasizes his being courted by the two figures representing metaphysical principles.

In the figure of Bianca, the allegorical scheme sets Eichendorff the difficult task of combining the most heterogeneous and even contradictory characteristics. As her name implies, she is to represent the prototype of pure, shy innocence in contrast to the bold, experienced, and mature Venus. But she must not be lacking in female appeal to please Eichendorff's active, passionate hero, who loathes the conventional. For this reason, the author makes her a charming and graceful girlish creature who blushes easily and is playful and saucy. Although these traits were not easy to combine, the necessity of having Bianca match the grandeur of the noble goddess confronts him with a more intricate problem. Who knows whether a character so constituted could have functioned in a book whose success depended on its being psychologically convincing? Eichendorff solved the problem in his allegorical presentation by suggesting mysterious connections between little Bianca and the holy Mother of God in allusions and hidden references interspersed in the narration and in the poems.

But this is not all. In order to show that a woman is a woman, and that the role she is to play in his life—that of Venus or of a Christian saint—is determined by the loving, courting man, Eichendorff postulates, above and beyond all contrasts and extremes, a kind of identity of the two figures at the highest level. This occurs during the masked ball held at the climax of the story and entails a sort of distillation or abbreviation of the allegory. The two women between whom the young hero is vacillating appear in perturbingly similar Greek costumes (in keeping with the Romantic convention of doubles), probably because Florio's imagination is increasingly captured by the ideals of the Classical world. Their identical appearance naturally leads to confusions unpleasant for all those concerned, including the reader, and is quite consciously introduced to symbolize life's inpenetrability and inscrutability. In the typical Eichendorff manner, these confusions are only resolved at the very end.

On the side of the good powers there are still two minor characters, who would be dismissed as "extras" in any other tale not as densely packed with significance as this one; here, however, they must be fitted into the allegorical mosaic.[52] We have, first of all, Pietro, the host at the masked ball, whose name suggests Christian symbolism. His relationship to Bianca, whose uncle he is, has a similar association; and since the apostle Peter is Vicar of Christ and this uncle assumes the role of father with the girl identified with the Blessed Virgin, the reader is encouraged in this interpretation. There is, in addition, his role as host at the ball representing life and his behavior towards the central character. "With a studied and expansive air," we are told "he questioned him at great length about his former life, his journeys, and his future plans." Such an examination fits the role of the future father-in-law as well as that of the divine leader which Pietro as Bianca's uncle and Maria's "trusty friend" must fill in *The Marble Statue*. With the additional remark that he looked so "observant, as if some special designs lay hidden behind all his refined words,"[53] the element of mystery which such a figure requires, is introduced.

Even harder to interpret is a servant who always appears at a significant moment, although he is kept quite in the background. In view of the dreamlike narrative style, lacking all reality in an empirical sense, one is tempted to take the events portrayed by the author for a visually projected psychological drama. The function of the servant would serve well to support this interpretation. He is mentioned three times, and each time he could be understood as the allegorical personification of the vigilant, cautioning conscience. His first appearance coincides with Florio's first fatal step. The youth has already met the delightful Bianca, his future bride; he has been taken under the wings of the experienced poet, Fortunato; and has settled in the inn. But something compelling in his soul leaves him no peace. The bewitching night casts its spell on him. He awakens from a troubled sleep in which he had significantly dreamt of water and sirens, melancholy and doom in the treacherous element, and is irresistibly drawn into the nocturnal adventure, in the course of which he encounters the fatal marble statue of Venus. In order to leave his secure lodging he must pass a "watchman," this very same servant; and he only succeeds because the man "lay fast asleep at the threshold."[54] Thus already here it seems plausible to regard the servant as the dazed censor at the threshold of consciousness;

or, in terminology less Freudian and more appropriate for Eich-endorff, as the Christian moral conscience which only when lulled to sleep offers no resistance to the imminent hazardous enterprise.

How right we were in not ignoring the fleeting appearance of this servant is soon confirmed when he is again mentioned in a very similar sense. The next morning, pale and fatigued, Florio must endure his mentor Fortunato's ridicule and rebuke for his escapade. But how does Fortunato know about his "lapse"? It is debatable whether the logic of the story demands any justifi-cation at all for his knowledge. It is significant however, that Eichendorff considered such a justification necessary and ex-plained it with the following words: "His outing in the night, however, had been observed and probably divulged by the servant."[55]

This repetition excludes the possibility of viewing the servant as an incidental "narrative stopgap" wanting deeper meaning. And he actually makes a third appearance in a function which fully corroborates our impression. After Florio has withstood the long, arduous entanglement and barely freed himself with the help of others, he decides to turn his back on the scene of these menacing temptations. In this connection, the servant is delegated a very telling role, as is expressly stated: "The untiring urging of his devoted servant finally convinced him to leave these parts."[56] Whose function is this quiet but unceasing warn-ing; and to which instance but the conscience can the influence so directly affecting the salvation of the central character be ascribed?

One is fully convinced of the allegorical significance of this watchful, but sometimes sleepy, servant, since the figure is used not only in *The Marble Statue* but also in one of his later stories already discussed, *Much Ado about Nothing,* where one is even more strongly reminded of Freudian theory. This conclusively proves that the servant belongs to the ever-ready store of images created by the poet. It is a dream once more in which Prince Romano gains insights terrifying and irrevocable this time, into the basic patterns of his psyche: he sees himself hotly pursue a figure whom he takes to be his beloved sweetheart. On over-taking her, however, he recognizes his "own horrible likeness." Had Freud known this passage, he would have been enthralled by the perfect poetic depiction of what he called narcissism: the dreaming ego must cross a doorway, at the threshold of which the servant is "stretched out as if dead." And this time, after the terrible revelation, it turns out that the servant is really dead, and his protective function ended forever.[57]

This, then, is how matters stand with the allegory in *The Marble Statue*. A young poet meets the two main forces of his culture, Christianity and paganism, in representative embodiments. He almost succumbs to the seductive, enthralling Venus, but at the last moment the strength of his good Christian upbringing awakens in him. He breaks off inwardly from the infatuation, and what had just been a magnificent Classical palace disappears together with its luxurious furnishings. What remains are the almost unrecognizable chunks of the wall and rubble. The hero is rewarded for his steadfastness with the hand of a pure virgin, mystically identified with Holy Mary, who has long been in love with him, as he has with her, though he was temporarily blinded by Venus. Thus seen, the allegory would, indeed, seem somewhat meager and wanting in substance, as has been contended in German literary criticism, particularly since Goethe's depreciatory remarks about this poetic mode. But we have still to delve into the greatest depths of Eichendorff's novella, whose real poetic quality results from a narrative phenomenon which we must now closely examine.

The bare allegorical frame is entirely clad in such a profusion of favorite Eichendorffian situations, poems, and landscape descriptions, humorous declamations, vivid genre scenes, and soulful moods of complete harmony that this story, above all others, conveys the impression of great riches. Around it the author has cast a net, more extensive than otherwise, of hidden clues and repeated words that can at best be adequately captured by the term *leitmotiv*. This is such a finely stitched tapestry that it would take much more extensive interpretation than ours to display the basic pattern. To save space we shall, therefore, refrain from pointing out the familiar *topoi* of Eichendorff's narrative world, such as certain atmospheric effects or the metaphysical, symbolic value of moments in the course of the day. Like so many others, this novella, too, ends with a gradual, stepwise disclosure of all mysteries, accompanied by the skillfully interposed phases of a sunrise. Like the majority of Eichendorff tales, the present one also makes use of the fresh, merry morning, the sultry afternoon, and the enchanting, ambivalent night. And here, as so often elsewhere, the essence of the true poet is put to the test; the deceitful Italy is first found alluring and then rejected.

Rather than tracing these phenomena, we want to turn our attention to three series of symbols employed thematically. While they are not exactly unusual in Eichendorff, they are nowhere treated with such thoroughness and virtuosity: we mean the motif of spring, the symbolic contrast of regeneration and torpidity, and the topic of the "old days."

The term "spring" is introduced more than ten times at highly significant points of the novella; each time it is most subtly related to the basic allegorical structure, serving to increase its depth and complexity. Eichendorff gives the reader an obvious signal that this is not simply a mood-creating background element but "poetic ideology." For the time of the story is not spring, as could be expected, but "it was"—as the first sentence relates and as the entire vegetative atmosphere suggests—"a lovely summer evening."[58] (Cf. this curious unrealistic combination of spring and summer peculiar to Eichendorff in the opening passages of *Taugenichts* and in our interpretation of the poem "Moon Night.") Innocently enough, the subject of spring is introduced by Fortunato in a metaphor on the first page. The more experienced man consoles Florio, who despondently declares his poetic endeavors to be unsatisfactory, in proverb-like words: "Everyone praises God in his own way, and all the voices together make up the spring,"[59] as if saying, God did not create the world in one day.

In his reply, Florio takes up the theme in a more profound vein: "Raised in the silence of the country, how much I longingly watched the distant blue mountains, as spring went through our garden like a conjuring minstrel, singing enticingly of beautiful distant places and of great, endless desire."[60] The revealing words "a conjuring minstrel" are as yet only used for comparison, and the term "spring" is divested of its full impact by the objectivizing "like"; but connected to the motifs of childhood, allurement, and longing, it is already being related to the central questions of the novella. One should also notice that the particle "like" justifies the usage of the verbs "went" and "singing," by which means the allegorization of spring is achieved.

Once again, Fortunato begins to speak. What he says is merely a rephrasing of Florio's words, but by dropping the word "like" and by retaining the word "minstrel," he completely eliminates the observed reality, the "objective correlative," and moves to the level of pure abstraction: "Have you, by any chance, ever . . . heard of the wonderful minstrel whose tones lure youth into the magic mountain, from which no one has ever returned? Take heed!"[61] With this statement we find ourselves transported into the allegorical sphere of the novella, and with "magic mountain" the theme of Venus is struck.

Let us review the progression or orchestration. First, spring is casually mentioned as if in chance illustration of other concerns. Thereupon the narration takes up the word in its actual, usual meaning; and by connecting it with other central elements, it becomes an essential part of the narrative substance. Finally, all the stops are pulled and the allegorized spring, personified in the seductive minstrel, becomes a leading character in the novella.

This very roughly defines the function of spring in the novella. From now on, the motif of spring is repeatedly sounded, varied, and deepened. We cannot and need not pursue this in detail, but can limit ourselves to a few of the most fruitful instances of its application. Thus spring appears in the two "framing songs" sung by Fortunato (probably influenced by Novalis). There the workings of spring, connected with Venus, simply stand as a symbol for the joy of life. The great sonnet of Venus makes mention of spring in this same sense, thus showing the goddess to be herself a power of nature whom no one can evade. This is achieved with a profundity, however, which surpasses most Christian poetic works in which ancient mythology plays a role, and the gods thus regain some of the dignity for which they were revered in antiquity. The fact that Venus chooses to characterize herself in a poetic form so artistically intricate as the sonnet, a form markedly different from the four-line stanzas Eichendorff prefers in The Marble Statue and elsewhere, reveals the foreign, artificial strain in her spiritual makeup which contrasts with her subjection to nature and contributes to the impression that she is a "torn" creature. The first stanza reads:

Why, spring, do you wake me up anew,
So that all the old wishes rise again.
A wonderful wind goes over the land
Sending sweet shivers through my limbs.
And the poem ends with the lines:
And painfully I must smile in the spring
Sinking in desire between scent and sound.[62]

One can now better understand what this myth of spring accomplishes poetically for the allegory. In connection with it, Eichendorff abandons the usual cliché of Venus, probably inherited from the Middle Ages, as a seductress of the senses who corrupts the soul, and reinstates her as Aphrodite, a lofty tragic figure inspiring mystical awe. This not only makes her into a fascinating, ambivalent main character of *The Marble Statue* but also lends the entire allegorical depiction intellectual earnestness and poetic depth.

In conclusion, we quote, for the second time, a passage in which the identity of spring, sensual pleasure, elementary beauty of nature, and Venus become obvious: "Tomorrow, tomorrow! He felt indescribably well. The beautiful marble statue had come to life and descended from its pedestal, the quiet pond was suddenly transformed into a vast landscape, the stars therein into flowers, and the entire spring into the image of the lovely one."[63]

The second topic, yielded by the dialectic of regeneration and petrification, is so akin to the theme of spring, awakening, and dying, that a separate treatment is actually not possible and an extensive explanation does not seem required. Purely from the point of view of plot mechanics, regeneration and petrification are represented by the statue's coming to life and turning again to stone (in this way, Venus is further identified with the spring and the elementary forces of nature, and it is clear why her helper, Donati, is introduced in situations of awakening and petrification). We have now sufficiently advanced to recognize in this rhythm a basic figure of Eichendorffian experience. The progression from the regenerating influence of the morning to the paralyzing effect of afternoon sultriness, and from the petrifying forms of a historical style of society to the rousing power of a revolution.[64]

Indeed, in the sense of religious history, from antiquity (petri-

fied but still living on) to Christianity—all of Eichendorff's
thoughts seem to be determined by this polarity.

These relationships are exquisitely mirrored in Fortunato's
hymn towards the end of the novella:[65]

When winds of spring are drifting
Gently over the green plain,
A hushed resurrection
In the valleys starts again.

Then something stirs below
In the still grave of the gods,
And man can feel the shiver
Deep in his own breast.

. . . . . .

Lady Venus hears the call
Of the birds' mirthful chorus,
And rises gaily startled
Up out of the flowers.

She seeks the old places,
The merry columned house,
Smilingly she gazes
Into the waves of springtime air.

But desolate are the places,
Her columned house stands mute,
Grass grows on the threshold,
The wind passes in and out.

And where are now her companions?
Diana is asleep in the woods,
Neptune is resting in his cool
Sea castle with its lonely echoes.

. . . . . .

Venus stands and ponders,
So pale in the light of spring,
Her eyes slowly sink,
Her lovely figure turns to stone.

For over land and water
Another woman appears,
So still and mild,
Enthroned on the rainbow.

The wondrous lady holds
A small child in her arms,
And heavenly compassion
Permeates the world.

There in the brightened spaces
The child of man awakens
And shakes off evil dreams,
Freeing his mind again.

And like a lark, now singing
From somber magic cliffs,
The soul will rise and struggle
Out into the morning air.[66]

Anyone reading these verses for the first time would probably not consider them much more than a variation of Romantic enthusiasm for larks and springtime. At best, he might be struck by the association of Venus with the Virgin Mary. Only after thoroughly studying *The Marble Statue* is he in a position to see that every word is a cipher in a magical script and that, together, they ingeniously spell out Eichendorff's myth of nature and religion.

Equally closely related to these interwoven themes is the subject of the source, which we would still like to consider. A few quotations will hopefully reveal its nature. When Florio first sees the marble Venus—and one should notice how inextricably several of the key motifs are intertwined—it is said: "Florio stood gazing as if rooted to the spot, for the statue seemed to him like a mistress long sought and now suddenly recognized, like a marvelous flower grown up out of the dawn of spring and the dreamy silence of his earliest youth."[67] Confronted with the goddess come to life, he fares the same: "It seemed to him as if he had known the lovely lute player for a long while and had forgotten her only in life's distractions,"[68] and already prior to this, Donati had bid Florio, "a former acquaintance, welcome to Lucca."[69]

What is meant by these assertions of former acquaintance and sudden recognition, by assuming familiarity with the world of Venus in childhood? Here again a psychoanalyst could readily supply the answer. The close connection between the psychic experiences of the Romanticists and modern psychoanalytic doctrines has frequently been stressed. To do justice to Eichendorff, one must carefully formulate his thesis that the delight in the sensual beauty of earthly life is innate in man as a creature of nature. It awakens much earlier than is realized; and no matter how far man may move away from it by virtue of education and convention, it remains for him a treasure of which he can be reminded all too easily—and be it only by the change of seasons or by the awakening of nature in the spring. At one point, Eichendorff has Venus express this thought with admirable clarity: "Everyone thinks to have seen me before, for my image glimmers forth and blossoms in all the dreams of youth."[70]

But also the counterforces are anchored in the impressionable childhood—a phase of life which is almost sacred to Eichendorff and, for that matter, to the Romantics and, indeed, to the entire pessimistic view of culture since Rousseau. Fortunato's singing in the garden would never have possessed the power to break the magic spell to which Florio was captive if it were not for a "pious old song which he had often heard in his childhood and had since almost forgotten in the changing pictures of the journey" (i.e., journey of life!).[71]

How can it be explained that the rivaling principles are equally rooted in childhood and adolescence? It seems that a phenomenon similar to the identity shared by the two rivals adored by Florio becomes visible on another level. For the protagonist as well as for the reader—and it would not be amiss to add: the author—these shared origins and appearances give rise to a tragic confusion of feelings which he can only master by an affirmative act, by *engagement*. Florio finds the strength for this existential choice. The moment he is able to pray from the depth of his frightened soul: "Lord, do not let me get lost in the world!"[72] the decision has been made and the entire, vividly sparkling scenery of Venus petrifies and shrinks into the paltry crumbled ruins of a wall. But the tragic element remains—we have already encountered it in another connection (see the chapter on Eichendorff's lyrics): the joy of life and of the senses, which the poetic human being must have for self-realization, belongs to the realm of Venus. This sphere, however, has been severed from, and rejected by, Christianity. Without Aphrodite, his vitality wanes;

without Christianity, he becomes depraved; and basically they are irreconcilable. This is the tragic Eichendorffian dilemma.

In respect to creativity, however, this schism is fruitful, as it engenders that field of tensions within which Eichendorff's poetic works could arise. Without the challenges and enticements of Venus, even his religious poetry would be doomed to insignificance. Artistically speaking, the merging of these diverse *leitmotivs* with the two opposing abstractions has proved to be very beneficial in *The Marble Statue*, too, since the thousand threads run back and forth between them forming a web of beauty in which life and poetry have become a unity and flourish equally.

Because of these interdependencies and ramifications, *The Marble Statue* is possibly Eichendorff's most closely woven story. Therefore one really cannot speak of "bare" allegory. Every sentence as well as every word has its positional value in the ideational structure of the entire work. We can say of Eichendorff's composition, as Thomas Mann said of Adrian Leverkühn's "Lamentation of Dr. Faustus," that there is not one unconnected, "free note"[73] in it.

III   Aus dem Leben eines Taugenichts

Models and Possible Interpretations

Every literary work is created within a particular tradition and is indebted to its predecessors for style and technique, for its form, its attitudes, and its conceptual framework. The novella *Aus dem Leben eines Taugenichts* would seem to have drawn primarily on three narrative sources: the German *Bildungsroman,* the fairy tale, and the Spanish picaresque novel.

The German *Bildungsroman* and its paragon, Goethe's *Wilhelm Meister,* which so radically influenced all the Romantics, has furnished *Taugenichts* its basic plot: an artistically gifted young man sets out in the world, goes through life's perplexities and vicissitudes (all of this strung on the thread of a journey which is sometimes interrupted but which never really ends), and ultimately finds his identity through the elevating and purifying love for an ideal woman. The *Bildungsroman,* in turn, had absorbed much of the tradition of the "innocent fool," a figure that has been repeatedly called to life in German literature since Wolfram von Eschenbach's *Parzival* and Grimmelshausen's *Sim-*

plicissimus and now passes on much of its character to the hero of our novella.

Of course, it would be wrong to conclude that a great writer would slavishly copy any such model. The critic who has once discovered such a prototype, only to find strained comparisons to it everywhere, is as mistaken as the critic who fails to discover it altogether; for he overlooks the main task of poetic imagination which is the remolding of tradition for its own purposes. Thus it is in keeping with the generally ironic tenor of Eichendorff's tale that the character of the Taugenichts is not gradually formed *(gebildet)*, but remains unchanged throughout. This can be seen when, at the end of the novella, he prepares to embark on his honeymoon to Italy, having just fled from that "deceitful" land and vowed never to return. Yet, metaphysically, everything has changed. The tangle of mystery and confusion has been unraveled, and he approaches his journey to Italy in an inner state of self-assuredness and clarity which he had not previously possessed. And so, on a different level, he does complete one of the basic figures of his model.

The fairy tale lends *Taugenichts* its folk milieu. This not only enables Eichendorff to assign his hero a considerably lower social rank and to make a divine rascal out of the miller's boy who with unabashed self-confidence gads about in castles of many lands; it also allows him to transform the "artist-hero" of the Romantics from an intellectual into the character type indispensable for his purposes: a man of emotions who is not even gifted with an articulate tongue but must, instead, express himself with his fiddle or in song. The fairy tale is the source of the hero as a country bumpkin who sets out to seek his fortune with no inkling of the world and who, despite or because of his abysmal ignorance, ultimately conquers it. Of course, our last remark too, must be somewhat qualified. In Eichendorff, the more obvious and cruder elements of the fairy tale are lacking. The miraculous, which earned the genre its French designation of *conte de fées,* has been transfigured into the marvelous in a loftier sense, and material reward has given way to its spiritual equivalent. Naturally, in Eichendorff's story the Taugenichts also gets his "palace" and his "princess," reduced though they are to a form more fitting his character and our experiences.

As a Catholic Romantic writer, Eichendorff was very familiar with Spanish literature, and a considerable part of his literary efforts were spent on translations of Calderón and Cervantes. Of particular influence on *Taugenichts* was *Don Quixote*. In *Taugenichts*, too, many of the perils encountered by the hero turn out to be windmill arms, figuratively speaking, the intention being identical in both books, namely to help the idealist triumph over a dull and uninspired reality. Even such minor but enhancing details as the hero's speaking in proverbs[74] were borrowed from Sancho Panza.

What specifically stems from the Spanish *novela picaresca*, however, is the main idea of a cunning rascal's ridiculing his solidly bourgeois but basically false society and, against all probability, triumphing in life. The Taugenichts even shares with his cousin Lazarillo de Tormes—the hero of the first picaresque novel—the fact that he first saw the light of the world in a mill. Granted, we do not find the bitter satire on corrupt social conditions, the sweat and the filth, the stench of poverty, the dogged determination to get ahead (by criminal means if need be); nor do we find the sharp, cynical eye which such a view would require, and the realism that shrinks from no horror. In avoiding all this, the qualities of the fairy tale and the metaphysical nature of the Romantic novella are of great use to the author. For time and time again it becomes apparent that by magically blending these elements—and herein lies his creative originality—Eichendorff has succeeded in producing the unique and immortal *Taugenichts* from three narrative worlds.

This tale, completed in 1826, is Joseph von Eichendorff's best-known work and—along with his poems, which were later set to music and have, by now, become almost anonymous folk songs—is responsible for his posthumous fame. It is also one of the most important and, at the same time, most charming creations of German Romantic literature. Indeed, *Taugenichts* was long regarded as the expression and epitome of the Romantic spirit as such, and as the most successful embodiment of the secret desires and longings of the movement which was so important for Europe.

In order to determine the reasons for this verdict, let us attempt to establish just what is "Romantic" about the story. First, the hero: young, amiable, unemployed, sensitive, and artistically gifted as he is, he represents the ideal of the Romantics, the man free of all ties yet universally talented. Born into very humble circumstances, but (thanks to his natural charm and luck) welcome in the highest circles, he is in this respect, too, the free individual who is at home in all classes of society but completely so in none. The Taugenichts' style of living is also important for this picture. He is a wanderer, who stays nowhere longer than he wishes, who, to the point of ecstasy, is at one with God's unbounded nature as befits the ideas of the Romantics in theory and practice. He is also eternally enamored and nonetheless manages for a long while to avoid the domesticating influence of woman and marriage. The image of the Taugenichts strolling down the road in the glistening, dewy-fresh morning and playing his fiddle to rival the larks has become the symbol of an entire cultural trend.

In order fully to comprehend the attraction and appeal of this work, however, our picture of the hero must be supplemented by additional observations. One very important layer in the novella consists of literary themes and motifs. One could say that the story is packed full of Romantic props, favorite situations, happenings and figures of the Romantic art of narration. There are the stage coaches and postilions, the gardens and castles, the elegant balls and excursions on country rivers, the peasants and philistines, artists and burghers, village lasses and countesses, embroilments, disguises, abductions and enticements, seemingly inextricable confusions, and yet, finally, the happy ending. The setting is Germany and Italy, as well as the ever-changing scenery of nature itself in its myriad of moods from all-pervading sunlight to the magical glow of the stars and the moon in the mysterious night. And from the forests sound the occasional calls of post and hunting horns, those acoustic symbols of wanderlust and the freedom of nature, which are the two characteristics most generally associated with German Romanticism.

We must also consider certain characteristics of style and form exhibited by the novella. That we are dealing with a first-person narrative is not decisive, although it was the Romantics who refined this age-old narrative technique to new effectiveness. Of much more significance is the ironic tone assumed by Eichendorff. In *Taugenichts* this irony, which has become the intellectual keynote of Romantic literature, is based on two different principles. There is, on the one hand, the Taugenichts' own ironic attitude towards his experiences, i.e., the superiority with which he pokes fun at the figures representing the *petite bourgeoisie* (the "Philistines" as they were called by the Romantics), such as the gatekeeper of the German castle; or his exquisite self-irony, which serves to allow the Taugenichts to soundly ridicule the wretched figure which he himself sometimes cuts. But another strain of irony, of which the Taugenichts himself is totally unaware, arises from the fact that he either fails to understand the world or misinterprets it. A subtle art of narration which enables the author to say more through his naive "hero" than the hero himself knows underlies this seemingly innocuous little story. This irony also presents the reader with a correct evaluation of the events that completely escapes the awareness of the narrator. And all this is accomplished without jeopardizing the psychological credibility and consistency of the work.

The significance of these two types of irony lies in sustaining and creating spiritual freedom. Just as the Taugenichts proves himself intellectually and emotionally independent of the random phenomena of life or of society by virtue of the former type of irony, so the author removes himself from the products of his own imagination by means of the latter. The result is a network of uncertainties and entanglements that can be seen through only at the end of the book. As for the Taugenichts: although basically he does not have the vaguest idea about the true nature of this wicked world, he is nonetheless so securely sheltered by his innocence and filial trust in God that no evil can befall him. Here form becomes an important means of expressing the intentions of the work of art, and a vehicle for conveying its ultimate significance. And here we touch upon another widespread interpretation to which *Taugenichts* has been subjected, namely that of national character.

The hero of the tale, it has been asserted, is not only a personification of German Romanticism but of the German character, of the German people and German ways, as such. This parallel has been most convincingly drawn by no less a figure than Thomas Mann. The very title of that work in which he expounds his theories on the Taugenichts contains the key to its historical significance: *Betrachtungen eines Unpolitischen* (Reflections of a Non-political Man). In this book, written towards the end of World War I, Mann attempts to prove to himself and the world that the Germans were not fighting for an outdated authoritarian system or for the brutal power of imperialism, as was maintained in the Western world, but that they were defending a worthy concept of human life quite different from that of the democratic West. It is beside the point that Thomas Mann completely reversed his opinions shortly after publication of the *Betrachtungen*. Significant for us, however, is the fact that the Taugenichts served him as symbol for an apolitical, inward-directed humanity, which, at that time, meant to him "German." In Mann's own words: ". . . it [his humanity] is convincing and exemplarily German, and although he is of modest stature, one would like to exclaim: truly, the German man!"[75]

To put it briefly: the German, as an individual and as a citizen, is, at least ideally, as unworldly as the Taugenichts. What is, or should be, of sole importance to him is his inner life, the cultivation of his heart and the refinement of his soul, an inner *Bildung*. He leaves it to other nations to rule and conduct politics; and—insofar as these obnoxious tasks are also required in his own country—to those whose calling this may be: the princes and lords, the money-makers and professional politicians. He, at any rate, will have nothing to do with it. Like the Taugenichts, he is utterly uninterested in the course of the world; indeed, one could even call him obtuse in this respect, for he is so very guileless and inexperienced that he makes the most amusing errors and becomes involved in comical embroilments. Yet for all his indifference to material goods and to the big, evil world, he reaps the finest reward: unity with nature and with the Heavenly Father, untrammeled security, and serene happiness. Whoever frees himself of the need for worldly goods, lives in a state of inner joy and, at the end, the necessities of life, or even more, fall into his lap. But, above all, he lives for love and music, where his true happiness lies. The most fitting motto for this artistic man are the Taugenichts' words to his fiddle: "Our kingdom is not of this world."[76]

It is not our job to determine whether this analysis of German civilization is valid, and although many reputable historians and sociologists maintain that some of the catastrophes in German history can be traced to a similar attitude on the part of the

German bourgeoisie, our only task is to establish whether this interpretation does justice to the novella.

There is something to be said for both interpretations of *Taugenichts*, the "Romantic" and the "German." They are based upon irrefutable historical observations and, what is more, upon quite specific passages in the text itself. However, those interpretations are one-sided. They do not sufficiently take into account that by the time Eichendorff began to write, the Romantic movement had to a great extent already exhausted its creative vigor. From his historical vantage point, he viewed not only the valuable intellectual achievements of Romanticism but also its limitations, its weakness and excesses, so that he was able to become its exponent and its critic as well.

No one can deny that in our novella the Romantic-German element exists upon one level; that—among other things—the Taugenichts is a symbol of a blissful bond with nature and of a vagrant life; that in ripping out the potatoes of the customs house garden, in order to make room for his beloved flowers, the Taugenichts impressively demonstrates his defiance of a society founded on diligence, restrictions, and precautions. He acts not out of arrogance or impudent desire to provoke but in the unconscious certainty of possessing the right art of living and the smiling approval of God. This, to be sure, is Romanticism at its purest. However, it does not mean that we may neglect the remaining substance of the novella.

Ambivalence

On closer inspection, we discover the very opposite of this unambiguous meaning: a principle of duality which extends into the structure and the plot, as well as into the symbolism and concept of nature, and which even affects the songs that seem purposelessly strewn throughout the narrative. However, to see this duality clearly, we must follow the developments of the story step by step, not just picking out random images, as is often done, but examining the connection of the various single elements to discover the underlying law, which only becomes apparent in the work as a whole.

Eichendorff is rightly extolled as a poet of nature. Mountains and forests, rivers and fields are his favorite settings. His indoor scenes generally have a negative function; and the first thing his characters do in the morning is to step to the window and take in the sweeping landscape. What has always been stressed about the Taugenichts is his closeness to nature, and to the changing seasons and times of day. This is so true that one can almost say that he is a part of nature or even a personification of its forces. Already at his first appearance we are struck by the peculiar effect of the seasons and varying moods of the day upon him. The melting snow and the sound of the birds herald the advent of spring, as we catch sight of the Taugenichts sitting on the threshold of his father's mill, wiping the sleep out of his eyes, as if he, too, were an element of the awakening nature. This gesture of harmony with his environment introduces him to the reader at the beginning of the novella, and the ability or necessity to mirror, in his own disposition, the state of the elements will characterize him to the end. (Of course, the Taugenichts is not alone in this. Observant readers of Eichendorff are well acquainted with the dependence of all his main figures upon the moods of nature.) To have established this, however, is not enough. For even in the first few pages, it becomes evident that nature is enigmatically Janus-faced.

The position of spring in the year is paralleled by that of the morning within the day. Morning is the time for venturing forth, when the Taugenichts starts his wanderings or continues them. The gleaming awakening of day and its bustling life never fail to awaken corresponding moods in his soul. "Above me countless larks in the clear blue sky—I was ashamed to cry out loud, but inwardly I shouted with joy and strutted and danced . . .";[77] "a few solitary larks that had arisen too early were already soaring among the streaks of morning, and the postilion took his horn and drove on and blew and blew . . . and I had but one feeling, that I had to go with him at once—far, far into the world";[78] "high above me in the air countless larks were rejoicing; so I wandered through the green hills and past merry cities and villages . . .";[79] "the lanky lad cracked his riding whip and galloped off, racing with the larks above him through the morning air into the sparkling countryside. . . . The skipper gave the sign and we sailed off in the glittering splendor of morning through the mountains down into the valley. . . . From the ship . . . a canary rejoiced and burst into song to our great delight."[80] These are just a few of Eichendorff's standard descriptions of the

awakening of life and the Taugenichts' delight in the breaking
of day.

All the greater is the contrast with the critical changes the
protagonist undergoes at midday. Noon is the exact opposite of
morning freshness, for it is a time in which life comes to a
standstill. In the blaze of the scorching, perpendicular sunrays,
plants and animals alike languish and die off. The Taugenichts,
too, is a captive of this force. These are the hours in which a
painful anxiety rises in his heart, filling it with melancholy. And
just as nature's other face comes into view when the sun is at its
highest, so the Taugenichts' soul is seized by thoughts of that
antipode to nature in his existence: his homeland. In the joy of
early morning, he had just said: "Now the village, gardens, and
church steeples were dwindling behind me." Gradually, however, nature's countenance changes. "But as the sun climbed
higher and higher [note the word "but"], as the heavy white
noonday clouds gathered on the horizon and everything in the air
and on the sweeping plain became so empty and sultry and still
above the softly swaying fields of grain, I for the first time
thought again of my village, my father and our mill, how cozy
and cool it was at the pond and how now everything lay far, far
behind me. An odd feeling came over me, as though I had to
turn back; I stuck my fiddle between my vest and coat, sat down
on the runningboard of the carriage and fell asleep."[81] Many
similar passages could be citied. Just as the Taugenichts is in
danger of succumbing to a mood of mere vegetation, his mind
begins to stir and he remembers his father, the mill, and his birthplace as symbols of his origins and traditions, of his family ties,
and of useful activity.

We can now understand the significance of nature's two faces.
The vegetative aspect is subject to a rhythm of blossoming and
withering, of animation and torpor, which also affects those who
live as creatures of nature. It is resisted, however, by their
ethical consciousness, which knows of goals beyond a purely
creaturely existence. The Taugenichts suffers from this dichotomy. Equally strong and legitimate forces—natural drives, a
yearning for faraway places, and moral obligation (homeland,
return)—struggle for supremacy within him. Following one force,
he must neglect the other, thus depriving himself of either life
or spirit.

We now notice how often the Taugenichts is actually sad (not just at midday but in the solitude of the night as well this feeling of abandonment can overcome him), a fact which does not at all fit with his stereotype characterization as the eternally gay child of nature. Every shout of joy is counterbalanced by moments of anxiety, and every blissful hour is followed by a fit of depression or even desperation. He is often frightened to death, dejected to the point of despair, and even bitter tears are not alien to this child of good fortune: "And all at once it dawned upon me that she is so beautiful and I so poor and ridiculed and forsaken by the world, . . . I could no longer contain myself. I threw myself onto the grass and wept bitterly";[82] and subsequently: "Just like this, I thought, the moon is shining on my father's mill and on the count's white castle. It is all quiet there by now, too. The noble lady is asleep . . . and nobody cares if I am still around or far away or dead—suddenly the world seemed so frighteningly big and wide and I seemed so very much alone in it that I could have wept to my heart's content."[83]

The most characteristic expression of these antagonistic ways of experiencing the world is two songs which, in view of the lyrical tone of the novella, could be considered as the two pillars spanned by the arch of the story. They are of special significance because the Taugenichts, childlike and naive as he is, does not (as we know) have a good command of reflective language. In his songs, though, he possesses a rare eloquence for expressing his every emotion, and we must listen carefully when he sings out.

The first song is the famous *Wanderlied,* now part of folklore:

> Wem Gott will rechte Gunst erweisen,
> Den schickt er in die weite Welt,
> Dem will er seine Wunder weisen
> In Berg und Wald und Strom und Feld.

> Whom God will grant his favor,
> He sends into the world,
> And shows him all his glories
> In hill and forest, in river and field.

Here roving is praised and even religiously sanctioned as a way of life:

Den lieben Gott lass ich nur walten;
Der Bächlein, Lerchen, Wald und Feld
Und Erd' und Himmel will erhalten,
Hat auch mein Sach aufs best' bestellt!

I gladly let the dear Lord reign;
The rivers, larks, the woods and fields
And heaven and earth he does sustain,
And has the best in store for me.[84]

The last stanza sounds just like a poetic paraphrase of the biblical word: "Therefore I say unto you, Take no thought for your life . . . nor yet for your body. . . . Behold the fowls of the air: they sow not, nor do they reap . . . and yet your heavenly Father feedeth them."[85]

It is interesting that in this poem the other pole, the opposite of the hero's gay carefreeness in nature—a bourgeois existence—does not go unmentioned. To be sure, it appears in a completely negative light, in all its misery and desolate narrowness. Indeed, his reproach of indolence, with which he ironically and comically twists the facts, even contains something approaching moral condemnation:

Die Trägen, die zu Hause liegen,
Erquicket nicht das Morgenrot,
Sie wissen nur vom Kinderwiegen,
Von Sorgen, Last und Not um Brot.

The indolent who stay at home
Are not refreshed by crimson dawn.
They only know of rocking cradles,
Of sorrow, worry, need for bread.

The very opposite sentiment is expressed by the equally famous poem about faraway places, which, once again, appears as a song of the Taugenichts. It is highly significant that this song, too, is preceded by one of his moods of anxiety, that he is singing "on a sultry afternoon" when it seems to him as if "everything had died off," and that it is explicitly related to his homeland and the mill—the latter by now unmistakably a symbolic image. "An old song . . . came to my heart that I had learned at home at father's mill." This time foreign places are negatively evaluated:

> Wer in die Fremde will wandern,
> Der muss mit der Liebsten gehn,
> Es jubeln und lassen die andern
> Den Fremden alleine stehn.

> Who wants to roam in foreign lands
> Must take along his beloved.
> For others might laugh and make merry,
> The stranger remains alone.

Again the opposite, the homeland is mentioned, this time as something to be cherished and as an object of the greatest human longings:

> Ach, die Heimat hinter den Gipfeln,
> Wie liegt sie von hier so weit!

> Oh, homeland behind the mountains,
> How far away it lies!

And the avowal ends with a nostalgic greeting to his distant native land: "Grüss dich, Deutschland, aus Herzensgrund!" (I greet you, Germany, with all my heart!).[86]

This poem markedly contrasts with the former, in which the Taugenichts still manifested his independence of others and his absolute trust in all-encompassing nature. In short, in the one poem, doubt is cast on wandering, in the other on staying at home. Thus arises the ambivalence which pervades the novella and demands resolution.

All things and events in the work are tinged by this ambivalence. We have seen that the Taugenichts' rovings left him happy but also melancholy at times, and that a sheltered bourgeois existence can be the object of his contempt as well as his desire. Nor are the other characters free of ambiguity; they too are subject to the law of double perspective. The gatekeeper, for example, seems, at the outset, to be the Philistine personified. His inflated exterior admirably houses his enormous inner banality. His first words to the Taugenichts are about his fiddle playing, for which he will give "not one farthing."[87] With the sure instinct born of antipathy, he recognizes in the vagrant player the absolute challenge to the respectable, settled way of life which he himself embodies. Still there exists between the Taugenichts

and the gatekeeper a relationship, a secret, unconscious understanding.

In order to see this more clearly, let us have a quick look at
the two castles which play such a key role in the book and illustrate the double narrative perspective. The Italian castle represents the appeal of things foreign, while the German one stands
for the power of the homeland, which seeks to win over the
runaway. Here the Taugenichts step by step is led through the
school that is to tame and socialize him, and in which he is to be
made into a "good-for-something."

In the castle, he is integrated into life by virtue of an appointment which he obtains almost involuntarily. "Thus I was assured
of my daily bread, thank God,"[88] he ironically exclaims in retrospect. His superior, the head gardener, perceives the character
of his new assistant through eyes that are sharpened by dislike.
He mutters something about "rabble" and delivers a pointed
lecture about the virtues of upright members of society compared to the shortcomings of the Taugenichts: he should be
sober and diligent and should not idly rove about or pursue
unprofitable arts.[89] These remarks call to mind the expulsion
from the Garden of Eden, where it was once said: "In the sweat
of thy brow shalt thou eat thy bread." But the Taugenichts is
still far removed from following this precept.

It is a fine touch that his first occupation should be raising
plants which, so to speak, allows him to remain somewhat longer
in his vegetative state. With his appointment as successor to the
toll collector, however, he considerably advances toward social
respectability. Like a prince with the tokens of his high office,
the Taugenichts surrounds himself with the insignias of the new
status: dressing gown and slippers, nightcap and pipes—the very
things which suggest slumber and domestic comfort.[90] But the
crowning jewel of his outfit is the fifth object, his magnificent
parasol, a device generally serving to shield the user from the
adverse effects of sun and weather. Let us call to mind, however, that in sun and weather the Taugenichts was once in his
very element. This shows just how far he has already deviated
from his original path.

Of course we know that, at this stage in his development,
these early attempts to domesticate him come to naught. The
Taugenichts rebels. First he destroys the potato field, turning

it into flower beds.[91] In a fit of insubordination he throws the
Philistine gatekeeper out of his realm;[92] and finally he flees the
scene of his short-lived conversion. The violin, which, significantly enough, hung on the wall gathering dust during this
period, is now taken down and reinstated in its old rights.[93] The
yearning for faraway places lives on in his heart, and he still
belives that he is not of this world.

Nonetheless the episode as toll collector has left traces on his
character. Even abroad he fondly remembers the dignity and
respectability he had shared in.[94] He had not merely exhibited
the trappings of settled life. His thinking as well had been
greatly influenced by bourgeois standards, no matter how ironically he might speak about it. After all, he had even considered
bidding farewell to the roving life and saving money instead.[95]
Small wonder, then, that during this period he even got closer
to the arch Philistine, the gatekeeper. The standards governing
the latter have also been impressed upon the Taugenichts, and
each time the moral voice speaks up in him or he is approached
with a promising offer, the gatekeeper appears before his mind's
eye admonishing him to follow the bidding.[96] If this were only
a mocking reminiscence and not a real possibility, the deep melancholy that engulfs him after such unexploited opportunities would
be inexplicable.

All doubts are dispelled, however, by the outcome of the trials
the Taugenichts must undergo, when the niece of the gatekeeper
becomes his beloved wife and the Taugenichts the gatekeeper's
nephew. That his newly acquired relationship is to take on symbolic meaning, as is often the case in literature (compare, e.g.,
the end of Lessing's *Nathan der Weise*), becomes apparent within
the context of the events at the end of the book.

This duality manifests itself in the general structure of the
book. According to the scene of action the Taugenichts' adventures can be clearly separated into two distinct phases: the
homeland (in the broader sense) and distant places. Once again,
we must deal with the basic conflict of the work. As long as the
Taugenichts is still in his own country, many forces conspire to
keep him there. As it turns out, a number of attempts fail to
capture and tame the unruly foal. The lad is not yet ripe for
settling down; he must run himself tired first. The Taugenichts
breaks out and travels to Italy. Here Eichendorff starts him off

on the second phase of his life. This would be obvious without
his explicit exclamation of "Now farewell, mill and castle and
gatekeeper"[97] at a time when these things lie far behind him
anyway and are little more than symbols for home and settled
ways.

Italy

The casual manner in which we are told that the Taugenichts
has set off for Italy, after castle, garden, and towers of Vienna
have disappeared behind him, may create the impression of a
random choice: "So I meandered on over green hills and past
amusing cities and villages down toward Italy."[98] In reality,
the choice of this destination is just as deliberate as many another inconspicuous yet artistically relevant stroke. Since time
immemorial, Italy has been the dream of all Northerners as the
land of art and of the sun, of freedom, and of sensuality. In the
course of Europe's cultural history, the contrast between Germany and Italy has assumed near-mythical proportions, and the
pilgrimages to the South undertaken by so many great Germans
meant something quite different in each instance, going considerably beyond a "trip." The land "where the oranges grow" (wo
die Pomeranzen wachsen)[99] is equally loaded with significance
for the Taugenichts. Indeed, this expression by itself conjures
up a literary model, Goethe's *Wilhelm Meister*.[100] Here this very
yearning for Italy is articulated in a manner, since obligatory,
in Mignon's incomparable "Know'st thou the land where the
lemon trees bloom?" with all its seductive and melancholy nuances. Certainly the word *Pomeranzen* expresses not only Eichendorff's dependence upon Goethe's work but simultaneously—so
much can a single word imply!—his distance from it. Just as
Pomeranzen in contrast to the standard German word *Orangen*
is unrefined, even crudely ridiculous, so the Taugenichts is a
scaled-down, folksy edition of his predecessor.

In any case, this journey actually represents the first time that
the Taugenichts thoroughly relishes his urge to roam, the absolute fulfillment of the irresistible impulse in his soul. However,
in yet another meaningful sense Italy is not merely a chance
destination, and Rome not simply the chief city of the country
he happens to have arrived in; rather both are the realization of
his great childhood dream. Italy is no less than that mythical,

distant realm itself for which his whole being thirsts; and the Holy City, which has hovered in his imagination since his earliest days, is the earthly incarnation of the world beyond to which he and his fiddle belong.

This is indicated in the same airy and casual manner as everything else important for our comprehension of this book, which, in Hofmannsthal's words, has its depth concealed on the surface.[101] On approaching the city of Rome, the Taugenichts recalls his childhood dream and thereby discloses to us what is actually the impetus for his wanderings:

For at home as a child, I had already heard many marvelous stories about the splendors of Rome, and when I would lie in the grass in front of the mill on Sunday afternoons and everything was so silent around me, I would dream of Rome like clouds drifting above me, with wondrous mountains and ravines at the blue sea and golden gates and high, glistening towers where angels dressed in golden gowns were singing.[102]

It is clear that here we are dealing with the child's religious vision of the world to come, expressed in fairy-tale images, as befits his age. Any remaining doubts vanish when the Taugenichts actually approaches his goal and sees the Holy City, as he now explicitly calls it, spread out before his feet. But it is precisely in this Rome image that the profound meaning of the ambivalence becomes apparent for the first time. For the Rome he now enters, and the experiences that await him there, are, indeed, as the reader quickly learns, anything but "holy." Rather than the city of the Virgin Mary, Rome seems much more to be the city of Venus, and it is certainly no coincidence that the Taugenichts recalls having once heard "that an ancient city and Lady Venus are buried here, and at times the old heathens still rise out of their graves."[103]

The Taugenichts, then, has also heard this legend of Rome. Which of the two views is correct? This is not the place to make a detailed study of the Venus symbol that plays such an important role in many of Eichendorff's works. The passage quoted suffices as an illustration. Here we touch upon the deep meaning of this tale, which appears to have been jotted down so lightheartedly; for it seems as if Eichendorff wanted to say: Rome is two cities in one. On this earth it is—as a city partaking in empirical reality is bound to be—a profane place, a domain of Venus. But beyond this, in a spiritual realm that "is not of this world" Rome is a holy city of eternal blessedness—the city of heavenly Christianity. The longing to wander, which draws the Taugenichts there, cannot be satisfied on this earth; indeed, it must necessarily be thwarted. Holy as the longing for faraway places is, it cannot reach its goal here below. Therefore, to spare oneself disappointments and to avoid temptations that might cost one salvation, it is better to stay at home and earn the spiritual realm of Heaven here and now.

But we have gotten ahead of ourselves. We have observed the Taugenichts upon his arrival in Italy and have realized that this journey will be a trial for him. If wandering and remaining a child of nature are truly the principles by which the Taugenichts should live, this will be proven in the land which is the incarnation of Romantic yearnings for the faraway.

What all efforts at home have failed to achieve is accomplished in the foreign country. His Italian experience turns out negatively, to be sure, but the Taugenichts is brought closer to his destiny. The dangers threatening him—isolation and loss of identity—are already hinted at in the song "Who wants to roam in foreign lands," but this lyrical-musical impression is enhanced by an image, as is so often the case with Eichendorff. We have in mind the Taugenichts' harried stagecoach ride through the Italian countryside, a ride that combines all the elements of the roving life as he envisages it.[104]

First there is the somewhat involuntary departure. (We recall that the Taugenichts does not exactly leave his father's mill of his own free will, just as later he does not leave the "very beautiful lady's" castle voluntarily but only after a kind of banishment or expulsion.) The Taugenichts' companions, on whose guidance he has relied, disappear overnight, leaving him behind. He runs through the corridors of the inn like a madman looking for them, but the stagecoach has already arrived and is waiting in front of the door. The postilion impatiently sounds his horn. What else is left but to make the best of a bad bargain? So he jumps into the coach, and off it goes. And, in the beginning, everything is quite to his liking. For a while, he still experiences the solitude as sweet freedom. He enjoys his newlyfound com-

fort, changing seats or stretching out to occupy the entire width
of the carriage. Landscapes and communities whisk by in delightful succession, people graciously doff their hats and girls
greet him at the window. Add to this the mystery of the unknown
destination of this fairy-tale journey and the purse full of money,
and life appears jolly.

Yet it turns out that the dream of freedom was only an illusion.
The journey takes over and the Taugenichts becomes its slave.
Wherever they come they find the horses already harnessed, and
he must continue, whether he wants to or not. Sometimes the horn
sounds in the middle of a meal. Then he must hastily rise and
follow the call, without knowing why he is being rushed. Pro-
tests are of no avail, for he cannot make himself understood, nor
can he understand what the people are saying to him. At this
point, his solitude switches from a sense of freedom to one of
loneliness. And when his seemingly inexhaustible purse, which
has become a symbol of his vitality, runs dry, anxiety sets in.
The thought of "voluntarily leaving" the coach occurs to him,
yet he cannot give up in this manner the vehicle which is to
bring him "to the end of the world." To make matters worse,
the coach suddenly turns off the main road, and the adventure
becomes all the more suspect. He has not stretched out com-
fortably for a long time; instead he is bounced back and forth
as the coach jogs over the boulders in the road. What began as
such an intriguing venture ends in a nightmare.

The impression seems incontestable that this description relates
to the Taugenichts' entire wanderings as a miniature portrait or
reduced mirror image might to reality. Such a concordance of the
smallest, seemingly peripheral flourishes with the central layer
of meaning has always been one distinguishing mark of the
symbolic narrative style; indeed, the presence of such minute,
particularly transparent parts—"windows" that allow light to
filter into the core of a story—can really be considered a criterion
for poetic creative power.

But what is now in store for the Taugenichts? His relaxation
after arriving at the Italian castle is only temporary—and the
nightmare continues. His initial relief at the favorable outcome
of the mad coach ride is soon followed by what seems like
heightened cruelty, in which menace grows into an ominous
sensation that his life is in danger. One can even say that his

alienation is at its height, and that if the German castle can be
called a school of self-realization, the Italian one can be viewed
as a torture chamber of self-alienation. For while the Taugenichts
vainly copes with the riddles of an insidious environment, the
reader realizes that in the castle the hero cuts off every reason-
able tie to the outside world and even his personal freedom;
moreover, he is completely robbed of his identity when taken for
a girl (and even the reader must wait until the end of the
novella to fully comprehend what has happened). This gives
rise to the absurd comedy of this selection, which, however,
cannot quite veil the gruesomeness of the mishaps. (We are
suddenly reminded of Kafka, for whom a symbolic, grotesquely-
incomprehensible castle plays an equally important role.) All
the more puzzling and weird must the Taugenichts find the
preposterous nature of the castle's inhabitants—from their mysterious facial expressions and the locked doors to the alleged
murder knife, and from the carefree servant girl to the crazy
student. His experience in Italy, his dreamland, turns out to be
a total disappointment. The coach ride, originally so jolly, becomes a frenzied hunt, and the hospitable castle changes into
a prison, from whose perilous custody he can only escape by
leaping out of the window.[105]

The Taugenichts' last hope is now Rome. His shock when this
hope, too, crumbles can only be grasped when we consider what
Rome had once meant to him. The gulf between dream and
reality created by his encounter with the Holy City becomes the
final and decisive factor in the Taugenichts' decision to return to
his native world.

The image of Rome, heavenly and eternal with golden towers
and singing angels, which, significantly enough, had first appeared to the Taugenichts as a vision in the sky, gives way to
the real Rome as he perceives it: it could be any foreign city in
which he feels excluded from everything and, ultimately, re-
pulsed. His yearning for the beautiful lady drives him to seek
her everywhere, and each new effort is a deception. The life
of the artists, its bohemian laxity, dubious morals, and Romantic
exaltation, serves as a warning of the dangers to which an extended sojourn would expose him, since he is by no means im-
mune to these temptations. (This part of the story contains
Eichendorff's attack on the bohemian life of Romantic artists,[106]

just as an earlier section ridicules the Romantic craving for the "folkloric" and the "national."[107] These thematic attacks serve to bring out his criticism of certain Romantic excesses.) In the artists, the Taugenichts sees the exaggeration of his own tendencies, a distorted version of his own being. Finally, an assault on his virtue is attempted;[108] this he does manage to evade, thanks to his naiveté and unsuspecting innocence, but it makes the prospect of any further stay in this city of Venus utterly distasteful. The decision to renounce his wanderings follows without delay, and we soon see him on his way back home.

Love

Before turning to the adventures that befall the Taugenichts on the way home and after his arrival, we must cast one last look at the central force governing his life, namely love. The star brightening the hero's existence from the time he leaves the mill and leading him on to the end is the beautiful, nameless woman. In the world of this narrative, the woman is assigned the role of a stable center which restrains the centrifugal forces threatening to dissipate life. The attraction keeping the Taugenichts at any one place is a woman: in the Viennese castle, it is the "lovely and gracious lady" for whose sake he tarries; on the road, it is a village maiden angling to tie him down;[109] and in Rome, it is the adventure with the noble lady from which he escapes unscathed due solely to his boundless inexperience.

This account, however, should not make us overlook the fact that women, too, are subject to the laws of this fictional world, and that even the gracious central figure is ensnared in the Taugenichts' spiritual conflict. The dual nature of the "beauteous lady" is revealed for the first time, by a strange reflection that appears to the Taugenichts during the boat ride in the castle park. "The lovely lady, holding a lily in her hand, sat near the edge of the boat smiling softly and gazing into the clear waves she touched with the lily, so that her entire figure could once more be seen in the water between the reflected clouds and trees —like an angel who quietly moves through the bottom of the deep, blue sky."[110] This reflection in the water suddenly conveys to us that notion that the address of "beauteous, exalted lady" used in the love song voices not only the Taugenichts' reverence for the lady of higher social standing but a religious idea as well.

The dual nature of the woman and her function in the tale become even more obvious in the description of the Taugenichts' dream in the farmer's orchard.[111] (In a certain sense, this vision is the opposite of the one in the castle pond episode, when she appeared as both earthly and heavenly creature.) Once again he espies his beloved, first in the "reality" of his dream and then as a reflection in the pond of his native village. Although she appears to be "many thousand times more beautiful" than in real life, she stares at him so woodenly that he is dismayed.

But this is not all. In the dream—a medium of insight highly esteemed by the Romantics—the spheres between which the beloved must mediate are clearly juxtaposed: nature and society, an esthetic and an ethical understanding of life. It is easy to discern the direction taken by the dream figure, which anticipates the course of the Taugenichts' journey through life. She moves off from the magnificent dream landscape spreading out before him, and floats towards his home village and his father's mill, which seem infinitely sad and empty to him. But the beautiful lady apparently considers it her duty to reconcile him with his homeland. Amiably she leads him by the hand, singing the guitar tune which enchanted him in the early hours of the morning. The symbolic significance of this action merits closer consideration: the morning freshness and the music, both long familiar to the reader as being synonymous with bright, flourishing nature and also as heralds of the world beyond, are now introduced into his home sphere. The dream ends with a double vision of his beloved: she appears both as a real person and as a reflection. This emphasizes the fact that woman belongs to both realms and simultaneously serves as a warning against losing oneself in nature. The woman is at home in both. She can be man's Venus or Mary, according to his state of grace. Only in the miracle of love, where morality and nature fuse, can salvation be found. Woman is the magnet whom the Taugenichts is compelled to follow, leading him homeward through all the entanglements of deceitful Italy.

Resolution

On the way, once more he encounters a mirror of his existence in the persons of three theology students from Prague.[112] They seem to be orphans; at any rate in the summer they must roam

from place to place as beggar-musicians while other students
go back home. The account of their life (we are no longer as-
tonished to encounter isolation and delight in nature as comple-
mentary concepts) moves the Taugenichts to tears and laughter,
and it hardly occurs to him that he is crying and laughing no
less about himself than his companions. But for them as well,
roving is just a passing stage, a facet of youth, for they are
students preparing for the respectable and secure profession of
clergyman (granted that, as theologians, they are seeking God,
just as the Taugenichts is). For good reason the refrain of their
theme song is:

> Beatus ille homo,
> Qui sedet in sua domo,
> Et sedet post fornacem
> Et habet bonam pacem![113]

Neither is it particularly surprising that even they, the Taugenichts' brothers in spirit, have secret connections with the castle.
Indeed, one of them is related to the gatekeeper, as the Taugenichts will be shortly—another sign of how much these friends
returning to bourgeois life have in common. The fact that all of
them are musicians of one kind or another—including the gatekeeper who plays the bassoon—should not be overlooked. After
all, did not the Taugenichts' dream prophetically show that it
would be impossible to persevere in the solid, respectable bourgeois world without that gleam of celestial music?

The ending brings for the Taugenichts the inevitable consequences of his decision to forgo the urge to lose himself in nature
and to wander. He has been tamed; love has harmonized the
two worlds in his soul, which harmony the author objectivizes
in the fairy-tale images of the hero's ascent. To the end his
childlike faith and trust in God never falters, and the rewards
for his steadfastness—the only virtue required in Eichendorff's
world in order to attain heavenly and earthly bliss—are heaped
upon him. The supposed difference in social class that almost
sunders him from his beloved is done away with. As a token of
the stability he has finally achieved, he receives a house, which
has assumed the proportions of a small castle, in keeping with
the fairy-tale style of the finale. Here life will differ greatly from

the village banality that has haunted him in his nightmares of a Philistine existence.

What actually happens is this: as if struck by a magic wand, the world lies transformed and, for the first time in the story, the magical twilight has disappeared, giving way to a welcome clarity. All the riddles are solved, everything that was left open is explained in retrospect, everything mysterious is unveiled, and situations that seemed inextricably entangled only a short while ago are now rendered clear and transparent. The gatekeeper loses all ambiguity and is recognized as the good uncle he basically always was.[114] And how consistent it is that the Taugenichts plans to travel with his young wife to Italy, to Rome, although only shortly before he had resolved "to turn my back forever . . . on that deceitful Italy."[115] For now the evil spell has been broken, and Italy is no longer a metaphysical force but merely a sensible, albeit enticing, goal for a pair of honeymooners. (Here, too, the song of loneliness proves to have been prophetic: "Who wants to roam in foreign lands/Must take along his beloved.") The process of subduing the unruly vagabond and "good-for-nothing" culminates in the playfully tender scene with the almonds he had brought back from Italy,[116] both as fruit and as an embodiment of his experience of estrangement. Love and domesticity appear to merge delightfully in the affectionate game of nutcracking. "And all, all was well!"[117] This final outburst, its resigned bliss and refusal to embellish life—intensified by the repetition it contains—can only be fully appreciated if one has experienced, along with the Taugenichts, the dangers he herewith proclaims to have survived.

IV Schloss Dürande

No less than all the other stories by our author, this novella offers the contrasts of forest and castle, love and monastery, city and country, seduction and voluntary submission—groupings which make up the unmistakable elements of Eichendorff's narrative art by now familiar to us. This time, however, these themes and motives are inextricably linked with a historical background —that of the French Revolution—so that the entire novella takes on a deep historical dimension unusual in Eichendorff. In an entirely new fashion, the reader is caught up in the resulting dynamics, as if he were suddenly thrust into life itself. One is reminded of Heinrich von Kleist's practice—which is odd, indeed, considering our gentle Silesian—and, in theory, of Erich Auerbach's *Mimesis,* where it is said that realism results only when individual destinies are connected with the flux of historical currents. In this light, *Dürande Castle* is Eichendorff's most realistic tale; and we want to utilize it primarily as a source of information about the author's attitude towards the French Revolution. Drawing on a fictional reality which is not only complex but is also sustained in part by subconscious emotions, can be more informative and stimulating than gleaning this knowledge from the frequent statements about the topic in the author's theoretical writings, particularly in his essay "The Aristocracy and the Revolution," a topic that occupied and moulded Eichendorff's socio-historical consciousness as no other did.

From our perspective, we are compelled to see in Renald, a hunter and gamekeeper in the count's service, the tragic central figure. Accordingly, the novella would be the story of his development from a servant devoted to his titled employer into a raging revolutionary, who kills his master and destroys the venerable Dürande castle. The story turns tragic because these deeds result from the best in Renald and because, in his destructive fury—which seemingly stems from pure righteousness—he falls prey to the arrogance and delusion known as "hubris." The entire composition and execution are so logically consistent that one could successfully apply all the concepts of the Aristotelian theory of tragedy, from hamartia to catharsis to the characters and events. Simultaneously, the poet expresses his condemnation of the French Revolution by depicting what led to it as a horrible, devastating mistake, even though an understandable, indeed a necessary one. The beginning and end of the novella evoke the "ruins of the old Dürande castle,"[118] so that— as in Adalbert Stifter's famous story *Hochwald*—the narrative events are framed in ruination as a reminder and seal of the personal as well as of the historical error. But now we must consider the portrayal in detail.

Renald and his sister, Gabriele, inhabit a hunter's cottage in the idyllic solitude of the forest. The paradisiac security of this house is underlined by Eichendorff's emotive descriptions: "One hardly saw it for all the flowers, it was surrounded by trees and clinging vines."[119] This idyll is disrupted by the appearance of

Eros, an appearance—so much may be said beforehand—complicated by differences of social status. Renald learns that Gabriele has a lover. One evening, he spies on the couple and fires off a shot. However he does not hit the nocturnal visitor, but his own sister who has tried to shield him. The girl does not know who her lover is; but her brother, spotting a pistol he has left behind, recognizes the young Count Dürande, who is not only his master but, to Renald's hierarchical-conservative mind, a ruler by divine right. Profoundly shaken by this discovery, Renald orders Gabriele's confinement in a nunnery whose prioress is their relative. His distress is understandable; not only is it rooted in his character and in his world view, it also stems from the fact that Gabriele was entrusted to his care by their dying father. This intrusion of erotic and social forces into the innocent world of the brother and sister starts the tragic events on their inexorable course.

If one wanted to elucidate all the aspects of the novella, it would now be advisable to examine the stages of awareness which Gabriele progressively undergoes in the convent. In this way one would discover that this story, too, lives from the masterfully created tension between mystification and revelation which is the hallmark of Eichendorff's narrative art. But as we are primarily concerned with Renald's story, suffice it to say that Gabriele, her entire being seized by the love for her nameless suitor, flees from the convent upon discovering his identity. Posing as the gardener's helper, she travels, undiscerned by the count, with his domestics to Paris, where he is to take up winter residence. With this, the first part of the story ends and Renald's path of suffering begins.

Renald is forced to regard his sister's disappearance from the convent as an abduction. In order to ascertain this fact and possibly bring his charge home, he obtains the old Count Dürande's permission for a trip to Paris. During this scene, the young man's misgivings are greatly increased. Although Renald makes no reference to his suspicion, the count proves to be completely informed. He laughs in Renald's face and his accompanying remark, "My son surely does not have bad taste,"[120] puts the stigma on the affair it had long possessed in Renald's eyes. This only reinforces the chain of evidence tightening around the fates of the three main figures. Let us also mention that

Eichendorff lets his troubled hero remain irreproachably honorable, being unlike the Count, who can only conceive of the whole thing as a lewd affair with, at worst, economic consequences. His cynical parting words: "Go right ahead. I do not want to stand in the way of your fortune; the Dürandes are always generous in such affairs; such wild young swans must be plucked, but not too harshly,"[121] are in crude contrast with the state of mind of Renald, whose most sacred ideals have been offended. What is more, they reveal the mental corruption of the upper class, serving to explain, with psychological credibility the coming revolutionary developments. Thus begins Renald's moving struggle for his rights which leads to the destruction of all persons involved and, due to its general disposition as well as certain details, has given rise to the very fitting comparison with Kleist's *Michael Kohlhaas*. We must now pursue the stages of this struggle in order to comprehend how the story of a young man looking for his sister and striving to save or avenge the honor of his family ties in with the historical events of the French Revolution.

Renald's first inquiries at the inn of a Parisian cousin bring him in contact with a group of revolutionaries. Eichendorff takes no great pains to justify his contempt for them. With no more weighty means than a few deprecatory words—he calls them "disbanded soldiers, idle journeymen, and like scallywags"—they are dismissed with a wave of the pen. Only for their leader, "a tall, gaunt man with pale, sharply chiseled features,"[122] does the author seem to hold more respect, even including such adjectives as "proud" and "refined" in his description. But although his aims and motives remain in the dark, he, too, is soon shown as a power-hungry agitator. His toast to the inn's servants, an ambivalent syllogism, is, in its mixture of contemporary thought and sophistry, pure demagogy: "You, the serving class, are suppliers of nourishment. Whoever furnishes others with nourishment, however, is their master; here's to you, masters."[123] Queried about his business in Paris by the Jacobin leader, Renald, in his desperation, alludes to his relationship with the Dürandes. To his dismay, the oracular words of reply, though couched in terms of social criticism, seem to fit his situation all too well: "That is an old house, consumed by amorous affairs; the death-watch beetle has already begun to chew at it."[124] The letter for Count

Dürande which the agitator presses into his hand is his means of putting Renald's private rancor in the service of the political movement. With the letter, the author simultaneously succeeds in motivating the later animosity of the young count, who draws from it erroneous conclusions about Renald's associations and intentions. In these minor details, one not only recognizes the accomplished storyteller, but is amazed by how keenly Eichendorff perceived the political and social psychology of his times.

In his confrontation with Renald, the young count can deny Gabriele's presence with a clear conscience, as he still has no idea that she is living in his house in disguise. And on hearing the admonishment of the "beggar-advocate" ("Take care. A friend of the people"[125]), he throws out the petitioner with his own hands. The author leaves it to the reader to imagine the feelings of the thwarted brother when, as if being mocked, he suddenly hears his sister's song in the house and catches a fleeting glance of her at the window. This novel, of course, has its share of songs functioning as important conveyors of moods.

In the following phase—Renald's vain attempts to enlist the aid of the law and police to secure his rights—Eichendorff does not spare the *ancien regime* in the least. He does not content himself with portraying the petty corruption of the lawyers and the indifference of the police towards a commoner lacking family connections, and he makes it very clear that in a state like this no one of low social rank could possibly accomplish anything against the stifling prestige of a ranking family, no matter how justified his complaint might have been.

Less convincing, however, is the author's depiction of Renald's final attempt—again as in *Kohlhaas*—to achieve justice by taking the last legal course open to him, i.e., a personal petition to the king. That the young Count Dürande happens to be among the king's attendants at that very moment is the kind of bad luck that is hardly compatible with the concept of an inevitable, inexorable fate. And that the count, like a petty court intrigant, declares the hapless Renald to be mad and has him locked away for months in a lunatic asylum only to prevent the king from reading the accusation which he anyhow thinks he has no reason to fear, is in gross contradiction to the otherwise noble personality of the young Dürande, whom Eichendorff provided with numerous positive traits from the stock of his own philosophy of life. Such malice is simply irreconcilable with the allegiance to home and country, the nobility of mind, and the very character of this nature-loving aristocrat who has just been a bit tarnished by the city air.

Is it perhaps the *royalist* and not the *poet* Eichendorff who was responsible for this episode and was ready to surrender the pre-revolutionary society to the severe verdict of corruptness, but not its august sovereign? Whatever the case may be, this political indulgence is also an artistic transgression. By his action the count incurs such personal guilt that every act of revenge on Renald's part seems now acceptable. Indeed, the revolutionary cause with which he cloaks his retaliation gains moral justification as the count's deed has made him a tool of the corrupt system. This was certainly not Eichendorff's intention.

The outbreak of the revolution and Renald's escape from the asylum mark the beginning of the last and decisive phase in the fortunes of the central figures. The scene is again the native province of Renald and Gabriele. In this section, nothing favorable to the revolution is advanced. Its fiercest antagonist, the young Count Dürande, disregards all warnings and returns home against the stream of fleeing noblemen, because "he . . . had no faith in distant places" and wanted to "honestly share in the joy and the suffering of his homeland."[126] The description of his visit to the convent (he, too, is in search of the missing Gabriele!) is loaded with open and veiled indictments of the revolution. The good nuns, fondly remembered from the first section by the reader, have fallen victim to the new fanaticism. A "Parisian commissar" had "quickly and cleverly arranged" everything, so that the pious women "were to don worldly clothes and go out to the cities, get married and be useful."[127] In their stead, a tenant farmer is running the convent estate. Not satisfied with this, Eichendorff showers him and his family with unpleasant attributes. Rather than being greeted by the nuns, a vicious dog lunges at the visitor. The tenant, a crude individual, kicks the dog. The dog whimpers, the man curses, inside the convent a woman is arguing, and a child is crying "as if lamenting that it was born in these times."[128] All of this has very little to do with the French Revolution; yet Eichendorff manages to credit everything to its account. Like the Parisian commissar, he quickly and cleverly arranges everything. But worse is to come: goats are grazing between overturned crosses in the churchyard, and blatant terror reigns, for "nobody dared to drive them away." The village itself seems deserted, because the shy peasants take the count for a "gentleman of the nation," but no sooner is he recognized than "at once all stormed out and encircled him, hungry, ragged, and begging."[129]

In this area, where the staunch loyalty of old prevails, Renald's journey is viewed in a correspondingly typical light. It is said that "he ran off to Paris and became involved with suspicious rabble and rebels."[130] There is no more extenuation of his deeds. The entire development has been based on the premise that he, once denied justice, now takes revenge into his own hands. But this aspect is no longer emphasized; instead, things drift unhindered towards their doom. Renald's ultimatum—obviously patterned on Kohlhaas' proclamations—that the count should "acknowledge and accept Gabriele Dubois as his rightful betrothed and future spouse,"[131] is obstinately rejected by Dürande, who does not even know where she is. And so the mob gathered by Renald storms the castle, "brown, slovenly creatures with shotguns, cudgels, and iron rods" who, unlike their leader, "are only out to plunder."[132] Too late the count learns the truth, that Gabriele had really lived in his house the whole time; too late he offers Renald satisfaction. The mechanism of destruction cannot be checked. Disguised anew as the count, Gabriele tries to shield her beloved from the disaster. Her efforts are in vain, and she can only share in it. Mortally wounded by bullets, they sink into each other's arms and die exchanging vows of love and betrothal. Again too late, and true to Eichendorff's proven technique of revelation, Renald now learns the real story. Renald symbolically disassociates himself from the rebels, whom he had recruited, by driving them out of the castle. In atonement he blows up the munitions tower, remaining inside to burn to ashes along with Dürande Castle.

When seeking to summarize the nature of the French Revolution as viewed by Eichendorff, we are struck by the following: on the positive side, the corruption and the indifference of the legal institutions are pointed out, as is the fruitless procedure of personally petitioning the monarch, depending as it does on arbitrariness and chance. The imperviousness of the system is intensified in the case of the hero since he is dealing with a noble family, which admits to affairs like the one presumed with cynical frankness and has apparently always taken for granted a certain erotic freebooting as one of its class privileges. Together these details, particularly in the second section, which takes place in Paris, clearly lead to the conclusion that Renald is not cheated out of his just due by mere coincidence or the wiles of fate, but that it is practically impossible for a wronged member of the lower strata of society to obtain public satisfaction in matters of justice; hence taking the law into one's own hands becomes psychologically plausible—a striking concession from a confirmed aristocrat like Eichendorff.

The clarity of this argument is somewhat weakened, however, since the blameworthy conditions have been completely restricted to Paris, the wicked Sodom or Gomorrah, so that the criticism directed at them merges with the polemic against the depraved big city repeatedly expounded by our author. Moreover, the élan of Renald's accusation is dulled by the fact that he is acting under a fatal misapprehension thus fighting for an illusory right—in striking contrast to Michael Kohlhaas, the creature of the uncompromising Kleist, who suffers bitter injustice, as witnessed by the outraged reader. One could conclude, from the circumstances pictured by Eichendorff, that had Renald restrained himself from the very beginning, his sister and Count Hippolyt would not only have stayed alive and gotten married, but the entire revolution would not have taken place or, in view of the loyalty of the rural population, would have passed over Dürande Castle without a trace. This conjecture could never be applied to Kleist's novella, for Kohlhaas *is* the revolution. While these considerations might not objectively contribute to the vindication of the general situation, subjectively they nonetheless have a very dampening effect on the feelings of the reader who is to pass judgment.

Any attempt to derive a justification of the French Revolution from the dire state of affairs in Paris as portrayed by Eichendorff is thwarted by the negative value he assigns to the concrete manifestations of the revolution. Its champions are, without exception, idle, lazy scum intent only on material gain. They are led by demagogic rabble-rousers who know how to pander to the baser instincts of the masses while indulging their own lust for power. There is no trace of discipline or ideals, or desire for social justice. Even Renald, the only revolutionary of stature, is merely fighting for his *own* rights.

Any remaining doubt is dispelled by the consequences of the revolution as shown here. The populace is impoverished and starved and, what is perhaps worse, intimidated by dogmatic terror. Those profiting from the new distribution are portrayed as uncouth riffraff. It is pointless to admonish Eichendorff that misery, despotism, and suppression had already prevailed *before* the revolution. It is typical for him to see these things as its *result*. One can think as he likes about religious orders and woman's role in society, the reader's sympathy has long been won by the quiet, hospitable nuns, and it is a blow to poetic justice that they are turned out of the convent. The notion created by a few cleverly chosen words, of a bureaucrat sitting in Paris, who, lacking all respect and human compassion, disturbs their peace and destroys time-honored institutions out of abstract, ideological principles, completes this negative portrayal. One cannot help but admire the storyteller's power to engender so forbidding an image. Only unconditional aversion could have inspired the many highly effective touches. One of these is the fact that the sole figure to be taken seriously has a primarily private rather than social iniquity to avenge and for this reason alone joins the revolutionary movement; that the injustice is largely imagined and Renald acts in tragic delusion, is the crowning touch. The last sentence of the story contains an admirable résumé of these complex ideas. "But you," it says, and it is not quite clear whom the author is addressing, "take care not to wake the wild beast in your breast, lest he break out and tear you to pieces."[133] In this final warning, the feelings of indignation that foster revolution appear completely stripped of their general social validity and are reduced to a low animal level. Their elementary, unconstructive might can even turn into self-destruction; and, through the choice of the traditional metaphor, their taming by the Christian ethics will be implied.

This just about covers the essentials, with the exception of one area not encompassed by our plot-oriented approach, although it seems closely connected with the problem of social upheaval and regeneration. Very often when the narration turns to the Dürande estate, a peculiar tone that is hard to grasp intellectually, creeps in. At first, one only notices its emotive value. With nothing

more to account for it than Renald's tortured state of mind, the
castle is shown in a repulsive light the very first time he approaches it.[134] The towers gaze "sinisterly" over the pines, jack-
daws "shriek" from the rooftops. But this is not all: the surround-
ings of the castle offer a spectacle of neglect and decrepitude.
The wall moat has "dried out long ago," "a marble Apollo with
a peculiar wig of ringlets plays the violin between circular flower
beds," "the forest, the old castle companion, was weirdly clipped
and aggrieved." These moribund Rococo structures, however,
are at war with nature: a bird whistles its morning song perched
on the toneless violin of the wigged Apollo, broad aloes "flaunt
themselves" above the helmets of the stony knights at the gate,
and the autumn does not fail to claim its share of the tormented
forest, coloring "everything a fantastic yellow and red."[135]

These curious observations are tossed in offhand, with no particular emphasis. Only when they are related to the central core
of meaning is the analogy revealed. For this is more than "menosprecio dela corte y alabança dela aldea" (scorn of the court and
praise of the village).[136] Does not this decrepit castle represent
the *ancien regime;* and does not nature take over the role of the
French Revolution by overgrowing and destroying forms that
have become absurd? From this perspective, additional significance is added to our previous observations. Beyond guilt and
justice, predilection and antipathy, the workings of an inevitable
historical process are here manifested, replacing the decrepit
and moribund with the new and young, At this juncture, it seems
to me, we have tracked down Eichendorff's actual sense of history. As the child of a particular age and class, he is necessarily
partial, but his poetic consciousness perceives the necessity of
change. This tension between his love for the old and the recognition of its overripeness permeates all the works of our author
and lends to this particular story a singular dignity. Its finest
symbolization is the death of the old Count Dürande in a scene
which is hardly connected with the plot and yet—in light of what
has just been said—expresses the true meaning of the novella, for
which reason the following excerpt shall be quoted *in extenso*:

Meanwhile the weights of the tower clock in Dürande Castle purred
on calmly, but the clock did not strike, and the rusty hand did not
budge from the spot, as if time had fallen asleep in the old court with

the monotonous splashing of the fountains. Outside, brightened grudg-
ingly from time to time by the distant lightning, lay the garden with
its curious tree figures, statues, and dry basins seemingly petrified in
the young greenery, which had already begun to climb gaily over all
sides of the garden wall in the warm night and wind itself around
the pillars of the dilapidated pavillions, as if spring now wanted to
conquer everything. The servants, however, stood on the terrace fur-
tively whispering among themselves, for one could see it burning here
and there in the distance. The tumult grew as it advanced past the
still forests from castle to castle. There, at the usual hour, the sick old
count presided over a lonely repast in the ancestral hall. The high
windows were tightly shut, mirrors, cabinets, and marble table stood
untouched in their places as in the old days, nobody dared incur his
disfavor and mention the new events, which he contemptuously
ignored. So he sat, in gala dress, his hair groomed, like an adorned
corpse at the richly set table in front of the silver candelabra and
thumbed through old history books, remembering his warring youth.
The servants scurried silently to and fro over the polished floor, only
an occasional flash of lightning was to be seen through the cracks of
the window-shutters, and every quarter of an hour the chime clock in
the adjoining chamber creaked to a start and played one phrase from
an old operatic aria.[137]

News of the French Revolution still reaches the old count, and
although his thoughts have already begun to withdraw from
earthly affairs, he still finds final words about Renald, who for
him has become the incarnation of the upheaval: "You do not
know Renald. He can be terrible, like a devastating fire—are
wild beasts allowed to run free in the fields? A splendid lion, see
how he tosses his mane—if only it were not so bloody!"[138] But
then his mind drifts forever from the moment. In a stirring death
fantasy, he sees his estate restored to youthful vigor and speaks
"of a large, splendid garden and a long, long alley through which
his dead spouse" was walking towards him;[139] and her image
blends with that of the Heavenly Queen: "She is clad in a cloak
of stars and a glittering crown is on her head . . . I greet you,
Mary, pray for me, queen of honor!"[140] With these words the old
count and the old order die.
  Compare with this portrayal the end of Eichendorff's treatise
"The Aristocracy and the Revolution" and its concluding poem.
Here a good deal of the vocabulary of *Dürande Castle* can be
discovered.

For the nobility . . . by virtue of its unperishable nature, is the ideal element of society; its task is to chivalrously preserve everything of magnitude, nobility, and beauty, however and wherever it may arise in the nation, and to mediate between the ever-changing and the ever-remaining, by which means alone the two can survive. Thus there is nothing to be gained from Romantic illusions or from stubbornly clinging to things long since outdated. This, however, seems to be the direction in which today's aristocracy is headed, to whom we bid a well-meaning farewell:

Prinz Rokoko, hast dir Gassen
Abgezirkelt fein von Bäumen,
Und die Bäume scheren lassen
Dass sie nicht vom Wald mehr träumen.

Wo sonst nur gemein Gefieder
Liess sein bäurisch Lied erschallen,
Muss ein Papagei jetzt bieder:
Vivat Prinz Rokoko! lallen.

Quellen, die sich unterfingen,
Durch die Waldesnacht zu tosen,
Lässt du als Fontänen springen
Und mit goldnen Bällen kosen.
. . . .
Prinz Rokoko, Prinz Rokoko,
Lass dir raten, sei nicht dumm!
In den Bäumen, wie in Träumen,
Gehen Frühlingsstimmen um.
. . . .
Lass' die Wälder ungeschoren,
Anders rauscht's, als du gedacht,
Sie sind mit dem Lenz verschworen,
Und der Lenz kommit über Nacht.[141]

Prince Rococo, you neatly laid out
Alleys lined by trees
And the trees, you had them shorn
That they dream no more of forests.

Where once a feathered plebeian
Burst out in boorish song,
Must now a well-bred parrot lisp:
Vivat Prince Rococo!

Wells that once had dared
To roar through the wooded night,
You have spurt as fountains
And fondle golden balls.

.　　.　　.　　.　　.

Prince Rococo, Prince Rococo,
Take my counsel, be no fool!
For in trees, just as in dreams,
Vernal voices can be heard.

.　　.　　.　　.　　.

Let the forest go unshorn,
Their rustling is not what you thought,
They have conspired with the spring,
And the spring comes overnight.[141]

What did Eichendorff wish to oppose to the idea of a revolutionary movement, in which he saw mostly the destructive liberation of base passions, and yet, at the same time, a force necessary to sweep away an overripe, decaying culture? The answer is given by Gabriele, the only figure in the novella who is not broken in spirit. Indifferent to the historical events and dutybound by her love, she abandons all earthly claims and unflinchingly sacrifices her life.

CHAPTER 5

Conclusion

IN the preceding pages the attempt was made to sketch a rounded picture of Joseph von Eichendorff as a novelist, a lyricist, and a writer of medium-length stories or novellas. Since an analysis in depth of a few characteristic works of art is, in my opinion, preferable to an all-encompassing, but necessarily shallow treatment which invariably turns out to be little more than an extended catalogue, I have been extremely selective in choosing the titles to be used for interpretation. But it should be borne in mind that Eichendorff was a productive as well as a creative artist, that is to say, a writer capable of producing quantity as well as quality. Especially in the chapter on lyrical poetry, I have limited myself to a consideration of a few songlike poems, hoping to capture Eichendorff's *manner at its best,* but without, of course, being able to convey the great wealth and variety of his lyrical work which includes short and long, secular and religious poems, simple strophes and complicated ones, and a great many sonnets, ballads, and romances, in addition to the *Lieder* for which he is most famous.

Among Eichendorff's novellas there are some that were either not commented upon at all, or at best mentioned in passing, such as *Die Glücksritter (The Knights of Fortune), Libertas und ihre Freier (Liberty and Her Suitors), Auch ich war in Arkadien (I was in Arcady too), Die Entführung (The Abduction),* and *Eine Meerfahrt (A Sea Voyage)*—the last two, at least, indisputable masterpieces. And even though his greatest strength lay elsewhere, it is noteworthy that Eichendorff was an epic poet ("Julian," "Robert Guiscard," etc.) and a dramatist, whose repertory contained historical plays (*Ezelin von Romano, Der letzte Held von Marienburg* [The Last Hero of Marienburg]), a comedy (*Die Freier* [The Suitors]), what the author called "a dramatic fairy tale" (*Krieg den Philistern* [War on the Philistines]), and other attempts at playwriting. Eichendorff was also the translator of Calderon's *Autos Sacramentales*, Don Juan Manuel's *El Conde de Lucanor*, and some of Cervantes' *Entremeses*. This accomplishment alone would have assured him a place in the history of German literature. Finally, we must refer to his numerous historical, political, and critical writings, among them his *Geschichte der poetischen Literatur Deutschlands* (History of the Poetic Literature of Germany), published in 1857 (with a marked Catholic bias, but written in a lively style and, in its details, full of sound judgments); a treatise "Der Adel und die Revolution" (The Nobility and the Revolution), published posthumously in 1876; essays on constitutional problems; and too many other items to be listed by name.

It would be absurd to claim that nothing new or important could have been learned about Eichendorff from discussing these writings at some length. But the principle underlying this book does not permit such expansiveness. It is meant as an introduction, and if it succeeds in stimulating the reader to delve more deeply into the world of Eichendorff in pursuit of his own discoveries, it has fully accomplished its purpose.

It is never easy to measure the impact of a writer on his own times[1] or on posterity.[2] That Eichendorff occupies a prominent position in German literary scholarship is an indubitable fact, attested by the many excellent editions of his works[3] and the long list of first-rate scholars who have explored and elucidated his writings for more than a century. I regard it as a special tribute to the name of Eichendorff that some of the best scholarship on his life and works has only appeared during the last decade and a half. When a poet can induce such creativity among his admirers more than a century after his death and in a country that has undergone as many radical transformations as Germany, then he is already immortal.

But Eichendorff's reception is not limited to the academic world. Many of his techniques and characters, most notably the Taugenichts, live on in countless imitations and modifications. A work such as Hermann Hesse's *Knulp*—to mention an author who has gained international recognition—was definitely inspired by Eichendorff's glorious vagabond. That Thomas Mann was an enthusiastic proponent of the Taugenichts and his creator is already known to the reader of this book.[4] And there are many other writers who were either influenced or deeply moved—who can draw the line between the two experiences?—by some aspect of his genius. Among noted writers of German prose and poetry who paid loving tribute to Joseph von Eichendorff are such illustrious names as those of Heinrich Heine, Theodor Fontane, and Hugo von Hofmannsthal. Occasionally, one also comes across a more unlikely influence. In a masterful essay, the recently deceased Walther Rehm, one of the finest students of German letters, demonstrates the far-reaching impact Eichendorff exerted on the famous historian Jacob Burckhardt.[5]

Perhaps the most important aspect of Eichendorff's suggestive powers are the many magnificent compositions inspired by his poems, virtually dozens of which were set to music. Through composers such as Mendelssohn and Schumann, Johannes Brahms and Othmar Schoeck, Hans Pfitzner and Hugo Wolf he has been lifted out of the confines of language and geography and has entered the timeless and spaceless world of music.[6] Some of these *Lieder* are today the anonymous possession of the people and have thus achieved the only immortality art can attain.

There are a few imaginative scholars who stress Eichendorff's modernity, especially in his treatment of history[7] and in his use of imagery paralleling certain twentieth-century concerns.[8] Some of their arguments are most persuasive. But I am not convinced that this phenomenon of "foresight" is necessarily a sign of greatness or that it can even be assessed with impartiality. Preoccupied, as we are, with the pressing questions of our age, we are apt to find them reflected here and there in the older literature we read. Eichendorff can pass the test of literary significance without it being claimed for him that he prophetically anticipated the problems of the future.

Eichendorff's true merits lie elsewhere. Of course, he also had his limitations. His motives were few,[9] the range of his interests was limited, and his intellect was not of the first order. His poetic world was small, but amazingly coherent and endowed with vibrating intensity, a goodness of the heart, and a vital joy rare in serious literature. Its lack of breadth is compensated for by depth—not the abstruse and oracular profundity that often passes for greatness in Germany and elsewhere, but the diaphanous depth of feeling coupled with serenity. Eichendorff is an unpretentious, healthy, and lovable author. In his prose writings he created not only a distinctive style and intriguing conditions of time and space, but also unforgettable situations and characters. In poetry he excelled because of his delicate sense of language and a musicality that inspired some of the best German composers. He was a past master of the short *Lied*-like poem, a genre which, in turn, is Germany's finest contribution to the world's lyrical heritage. From a broad international point of view, taking into account his shortcomings as well as his merits and accomplishments, Joseph von Eichendorff can be characterized as a great minor poet[10] worthy of a prominent place in world literature.

Notes and References

Preface

1. Chapter 4, pp. 131-132.
2. Oskar Seidlin, *Versuche über Eichendorff* (Göttingen Vandenhoeck & Ruprecht, 1965), p. 129.

Acknowledgments

1. *JEGP,* LVI (1957), 542-49.
2. *EG,* XII (1957), 18-33.
3. *"Nachwort"* in *Aus dem Leben eines Taugenichts* (New York: McGraw-Hill, 1969).

Chapter One

1. For a brilliant explanation of the role which the Rococo plays in Eichendorff, see Walther Rehm, "Prinz Rokoko im alten Garten: Eine Eichendorffstudie" in *Späte Studien* (Berne, 1964), pp. 122-214.
2. "Eichendorff's Persönlichkeit" in *Eichendorff heute,* ed. Paul Stöcklein (Munich, 1960), pp. 242-43.
3. *Werke: Erzählende Dichtungen, Vermischte Schriften* (Stuttgart: Cotta, 1953), pp. 54-55. All future page references are to this edition of Eichendorff's prose writings. All translations are my own. See also Paul Stöcklein, *Joseph von Eichendorff in Selbstzeugnissen und Bilddokumenten* (Hamburg: Rowohlt, 1963).
4. *Werke: Gedichte, Epen, Dramen* (Stuttgart: Cotta, 1953), p. 112. All future references to Eichendorff's poetry are taken from this volume. Translations are my own.
5. *Ibid.,* p. 57.
6. See also the discussion of the poem "Die zwei Gesellen" (The Two Companions) in Chapter 3, pp. 80-85.
7. Cf. the section on *Schloss Dürande* in Chapter 5.
8. For a full account see Gerhard Möbus, *Eichendorff in Heidelberg: Wirkungen einer Begegnung* (Düsseldorf: Diedrich, 1954).
9. *Die grossen Deutschen: Deutsche Biographie,* ed. H. Heimpel *et al.* (Berlin: Ullstein, 1956), III, 106-116.
10. *Ibid.,* p. 111.

11. For details on Eichendorff's career as an official, consult Hans Pörnbacher, "Joseph von Eichendorff als Beamter, dargestellt auf Grund bisher unbekannter Akten," Diss. Frankfurt a.M., 1964. 104 pp.

Chapter Two

1. *Erzählende Dichtungen*, pp. 98-99.
2. See Chapter 1, p. 20.
3. *Op. cit.*, p. 217.
4. Cf. the section on *Viel Lärmen um nichts* in Chapter 5.
5. *Op. cit.*, p. 294.
6. *Ibid.*, p. 46.
7. *Ibid.*, p. 9.
8. *Ibid.*, p. 33.
9. *Ibid.*, p. 63.
10. Oskar Seidlin, *op. cit.*, prefers the expression "emblematic" (see pp. 34 and 282). Cf. also Helmut Rehder, "Ursprünge dichterischer Emblematik in Eichendorffs Prosawerk," *JEGP*, LVI (1957), 528-41 and Bengt A. Sörensen, "Zum Problem des Symbolischen und Allegorischen in Eichendorffs epischen Bilderstil," *ZfdPh*, LXXXV (1966), 598-606. Walter Benjamin, in his book *Ursprung des deutschen Trauerspiels* (Berlin: Rowohlt, 1928), especially in the last chapter (pp. 155 ff.), condemns the customary deprecation of the "allegorical" mode. Hans-Georg Gadamer also pleads for a revision of the traditional distinctions between "symbolic" and "allegorical" in his *Wahrheit und Methode: Grundzüge einer philosophischen Hermeneutik* (Tübingen: Mohr, 1960), pp. 155 ff.
11. *Op. cit.*, p. 9.
12. *Ibid.*, pp. 9-10.
13. Cf. Bernhard Blume, "Die Kahnfahrt. Ein Beitrag zur Motivgeschichte des 18. Jahrhunderts," in *Euphorion*, LI (1957), 355-84.
14. Cf. Detlev W. Schumann, "Some Scenic Motifs in Eichendorff's *Ahnung und Gegenwart*," in *JEGP* LVI (1957), 550-69, especially pp. 551 and 557-58.
15. *Op. cit.*, p. 288.
16. *Ibid.*, p. 129.
17. *Ibid.*, p. 135.
18. *Ibid.*, p. 140.
19. *Ibid.*, p. 135.
20. *Ibid.*, p. 140.
21. *Ibid.*
22. *Ibid.*, p. 138.
23. *Ibid.*, p. 135.
24. *Ibid.*, p. 146.

25. *Ibid.*, p. 148.
26. *Ibid.*, p. 155.
27. *Ibid.*, p. 156.
28. *Ibid.*, p. 157.
29. *Ibid.*, p. 158.
30. *Ibid.*, p. 159-60.
31. E.g. in *Das Marmorbild,* p. 336.
32. *Op. cit.*, p. 160.
33. *Ibid.*, pp. 48 ff.
34. *Ibid.*, p. 160.
35. *Ibid.*, p. 189.
36. Cf. Paul Requadt, "Eichendorffs Italien," *Die Bildersprache der deutschen Italiendichtung* in (Berne: Francke 1962), pp. 107-25.
37. Thomas A. Riley, in his article "An Allegorical Interpretation of Eichendorff's *Ahnung und Gegenwart*" in *The Modern Language Review* LIV (1959), 204-13, shows what kind of historical themes Eichendorff is trying to allegorize in this novel.
38. The four volumes of Jean Paul's novel *Titan* had appeared between 1800 and 1803. Ludwig Tieck's *Franz Sternbalds Wanderungen,* the prototype of the Romantic *Künstlerroman,* existed since 1798. Clemens Brentano's novel *Godwi* was published in 1800, and the famous *Heinrich von Ofterdingen,* by Novalis (Friedrich Leopold von Hardenberg), in which the "Blue Flower," destined to become the symbol of German Romanticism, is introduced, was written in 1800 and published posthumously by Friedrich Schlegel and Ludwig Tieck in 1802.
39. Otto Friedrich Bollnow, "Das romantische Weltbild bei Eichendorff," in *Unruhe und Geborgenheit im Weltbild neuerer Dichter* (Stuttgart; Kohlhammer, 1953), pp. 227-59; originally in *Die Sammlung* VI (1951), 456-69, 518-27.
40. See the section on *Viel Lärmen um nichts* in Chapter 4.
41. For a detailed discussion of Eichendorff's atmospheric symbolism the reader is referred to Chapter 4, especially the section on *Taugenichts,* pp. 134-135. Cf. also Peter Schwarz, "Die Bedeutung der Tageszeiten in der Dichtung Eichendorffs: Studien zu Eichendorffs Motivik, Erzählstruktur, Zeitbegriff und Ästhetik auf geistesgeschichtlicher Grundlage" (Diss. Freiburg, 1964).
42. "Eine Landschaft Eichendorffs," in *Euphorion* LI (1957), 42-60, reprinted in *Eichendorff heute,* ed. Paul Stöcklein (Munich: Bayerischer Schulbuch-Verlag, 1960), pp. 19-43. See also Leo Spitzer, "Zu einer Landschaft Eichendorffs," in *Euphorion* (1958), 142-52.
43. *Op. cit.*, p. 441.
44. Spitzer, *loc. cit.*, p. 148.
45. *Op. cit.*, p. 303.

46. *Ibid.*, p. 96.

47. *Ibid.*, p. 40.

48. *Ibid.*, p. 61.

49. *Ibid.*, p. 17.

50. *Ibid.*, p. 152.

51. See Chapter 1, p. 15.

52. *Op. cit.*, p. 30. The most comprehensive among the many works about Eichendorff's poetics is Hans Jürg Lüthi's *Dichtung und Dichter bei Joseph von Eichendorff* (Berne and Munich: Francke, 1966).

53. *Op. cit.*, p. 30.

54. *Ibid.*, p. 32.

55. *Ibid.*

56. *Ibid.*, p. 31.

57. "Alas, so little is accomplished with verses if you write them early. One ought to wait with them, gathering meaning and sweetness throughout a whole life, a long one if possible, and then, quite in the end, maybe one could write ten lines that are good." *Die Aufzeichnungen des Malte Laurids Brigge* in Rainer Maria Rilke, *Sämtliche Werke* (Frankfurt: Insel-Verlag, 1966), VI, 723-24. The translation is my own.

58. *Op. cit.*, p. 31-32.

59. It has also been said that Friedrich Schlegel was a model for Faber.

60. *Op. cit.*, p. 31.

61. *Ibid.*, p. 26.

62. *Ibid.*, p. 31.

63. *Ibid.*, p. 30.

64. *Ibid.*, p. 31.

65. *Ibid.*, p. 32.

66. *Ibid.*

67. *Ibid.*, p. 30.

68. In this section, Eichendorff makes specific allusions to literary personalities and fashions of his day. Cf. the notes on pp. 502-12 of *Sämtliche Werke des Freiherrn Joseph von Eichendorff*, vol. 3: *Ahnung und Gegenwart*, ed. W. Kosch and M. Speyer (Regensburg, n.d.). Since these are of interest only to the historian of German literature, my discussion of them is couched in the most general terms.

69. *Op. cit.*, pp. 65-66.

70. August Lafontaine (1758-1831), a prolific popular novelist, born in Germany of French extraction, author of 160 books.

71. *Op. cit.*, p. 146.

72. *Ibid.*

73. *Ibid.*, p. 145.

74. Book Two, chapter twelve.

75. *Op. cit.,* p. 145.

76. *Ibid.,* p. 146.

77. *Ibid.,* p. 132.

78. *Ibid.*

79. *Ibid.* Cf. Theodore Ziolkowski's article "Der Karfunkelstein" in *Euphorion* LV (1961), 297-236.

80. *Op. cit.,* p. 134.

81. *Ibid.*

82. *Ibid.*

83. *Ibid.,* pp. 129-30.

84. *Ibid.,* p. 130.

85. *Ibid.,* p. 141.

86. *Ibid.,* p. 297.

87. *Ibid.,* pp. 72-73.

88. *Ibid.,* p. 73.

89. *Ibid.,* p. 165.

90. *Ibid.*

91. *Ibid.,* p. 166.

92. *Ibid.,* p. 167.

93. *Ibid.,* p. 62.

94. *Ibid.,* p. 172. Cf. the discussion of *Schloss Dürande* in Chapter 4, especially pp. 157-161.

95. Cf. Ingeborg-Maria Porsch, "Die Macht des vergangenen Lebens in "Eichendorffs Roman *Ahnung und Gegenwart*" (Diss. Frankfurt, 1951).

96. *Op. cit.,* pp. 296-297.

Chapter Three

1. Josef Nadler's book, *Eichendorffs Lyrik, ihre Technik und ihre Geschichte* (Prague, 1908) (Prager deutsche Studien, No. 10) attempts to treat Eichendorff's poetry comprehensively. There are many specialized studies concerning Eichendorff's lyrical oeuvre, such as Rudolf Haller's *Eichendorffs Balladenwerk* (Berne and Munich: Francke, 1962) and Hans Wolffheim's *Sinn und Deutung der Sonett-Gestaltung im Werk Eichendorffs* (Diss. Hamburg), (Bremen, 1933). The number of interpretations of individual poems, as well as studies of themes and motifs, is large.

2. *Eichendorff Werke: Gedichte, Epen, Dramen,* pp. 63-64.

3. For a treatment of this poem and "Frische Fahrt" (Brisk Journey) from this point of view, see Bernhard Blume, "Das Bild des Schiffbruchs in der Romantik," in *Jahrbuch der deutschen Schillergesellschaft* XI (1958), especially pp. 149-50.

4. To stagnate and to lose oneself to the world. Cf. Chapter 1, p. 18.

5. *Op. cit.*, p. 9.

6. It is significant that these verses are placed in the mouth of Countess Romana, the Venus figure in *Ahnung und Gegenwart,* whose dissipated life ends in suicide. See *Erzählende Dichtungen,* pp. 124-25.

7. See Chapter 2, p. 59.

8. For both "wirren" and "Aurora" also consult the section in *Viel Lärmen um nichts* in the following chapter.

9. This poem opens Chapter I, Book III, of Johann Wolfgang Goethe's novel *Wilhelm Meisters Lehrjahre.*

10. Translation with minor changes from *The Penguin Book of German Verse,* ed. Leonard Foster (Baltimore, 1964) pp. 216-17.

11. *Op. cit.*, p. 35.

12. Oskar Seidlin, *loc. cit.* pp. 54 ff, has supplied such an analysis in extensive and admirable detail. In the same book, he deals with "Die zwei Gesellen" on pp. 161 ff.

13. *Op. cit.*, p. 306.

Chapter Four

1. For example, Walter Pabst, "Die Theorie der Novelle in Deutschland" in *Romanistisches Jahrbuch* II (1949), 81-124, and Bernhard von Arx, *Novellistisches Dasein: Spielraum einer Gattung in der Goethezeit* (Zürich: Artemis-Verlag, 1953).

2. *Werke: Erzählende Dichtungen,* p. 441.

3. *Ibid.,* p. 500.

4. *Ibid.,* p. 495.

5. *Ibid.*

6. *Ibid.,* p. 303.

7. *Das Marmorbild, ibid.,* p. 19.

8. *Dichter und ihre Gesellen, ibid.,* p. 728.

9. *Eine Meerfahrt, ibid.,* p. 807.

10. *Auch ich war in Arkadien, ibid.,* p. 728.

11. *Ibid.,* p. 497.

12. *Ibid.,* p. 498.

13. *Ibid.*

14. *Ibid.*

15. *Ibid.,* p. 499.

16. *Ibid.*

17. *Ibid.*

18. *Ibid.,* p. 728.

19. *Ibid.,* p. 505.

20. *Ibid.,* p. 307.

21. *Ibid.,* p. 853.

22. *Ibid.*, p. 899.

23. *Ibid.*, p. 437.

24. *Ibid.*, p. 485.

25. *Ibid.*, p. 435.

26. *Auch ich war in Arkadien, ibid.*, p. 748.

27. *Aus dem Leben eines Taugenichts, ibid.*, p. 433.

28. *Auch ich war in Arkadien, ibid.*, p. 748.

29. *Ibid.*, p. 484.

30. *Die Glücksritter, ibid.*, p. 937.

31. *Das Marmorbild, ibid.*, p. 356.

32. *Aus dem Leben eines Taugenichts, ibid.*, p. 434.

33. *Ibid.*, p. 327.

34. *Ibid.*, p. 345.

35. *Ibid.*, p. 322.

36. *Ibid.*, p. 324.

37. *Ibid.*, p. 323.

38. Berthold Wiese und Erasmo Pèrcopo, *Geschichte der Italienischen Literatur* (Leipzig and Vienna: Bibliographisches Institut, 1910), p. 178.

39. p. 314.

40. p. 323.

41. *Ibid.*, p. 313.

42. *Ibid.*

43. *Ibid.*, p. 314.

44. *Ibid.*, p. 334.

45. *Ibid.*, p. 338.

46. *Ibid.*, p. 313.

47. *Ibid.*, p. 325.

48. *Ibid.*

49. *Ibid.*

50. *Ibid.*, p. 308.

51. *Ibid.*, p. 315.

52. Cf. Egon Schwarz, "Ein Beitrag zur allegorischen Deutung von Eichendorffs Novelle "Das Marmorbild," *Monatshefte*, XLVIII (1956), 215-20.

53. *Op. cit.*, p. 330.

54. *Ibid.*, p. 316.

55. *Ibid.*, p. 319.

56. *Ibid.*, p. 341.

57. *Ibid.*, pp. 460-61.

58. *Ibid.*, p. 307.

59. *Ibid.*

60. *Ibid.*, p. 308.

61. *Ibid.*

62. *Ibid.*, p. 322.

63. *Ibid.*, p. 324.

64. See the section on *Dürande Castle*, in Chapter 4, pp. 149-169.

65. Cf. also the prose passage following Fortunato's hymn on p. 344.

66. *Op. cit.*, pp. 342-43.

67. *Ibid.*, p. 318.

68. *Ibid.*, p. 323.

69. *Ibid.*, p. 314. Also p. 337, where Florio is struck by the remembrance "that he had often seen such a picture at home in his early childhood, a wonderfully beautiful lady in the same attire, with a knight at her feet and behind them a spacious garden with many fountains and artfully clipped alleys."

70. *Ibid.*, p. 338.

71. *Ibid.*, p. 336.

72. *Ibid.*, p. 338.

73. *Dr. Faustus* (New York: The Modern Library, n.d.), p. 486.

74. *Op. cit.*, pp. 353 and 375.

75. Thomas Mann, "Von der Tugend," *Betrachtungen eines Unpolitischen* (Berlin, 1918), p. 372.

76. *Op. cit.*, p. 368.

77. *Ibid.*, p. 351.

78. *Ibid.*, pp. 361-62.

79. *Ibid.*, p. 368.

80. *Ibid.*, p. 421.

81. *Ibid.*, p. 351.

82. *Ibid.*, p. 357.

83. *Ibid.*, p. 375. This thesis is also advanced in Josef Kunz's book, *Eichendorff. Höhepunkt und Krise der Spätromantik* (Oberursel, 1951).

84. *Ibid.*, p. 350.

85. Matthew 6:25-26.

86. *Op. cit.*, p. 393.

87. *Ibid.*, p. 352.

88. *Ibid.*

89. *Ibid.*

90. *Ibid.*, p. 358.

91. *Ibid.*, p. 359.

92. *Ibid.*, p. 360.

93. *Ibid.*, p. 368.

94. *Ibid.*, p. 371.

95. *Ibid.*, p. 359.

96. *Ibid.*, p. 375.

97. *Ibid.*, p. 380.

98. *Ibid.*, p. 368.

99. *Ibid.*, p. 369.

100. Cf. Chapter 3, pp. 91 ff.

101. *Aufzeichnungen*, ed. H. Steiner (Frankfurt: S. Fischer, 1959), p. 47.

102. *Op. cit.*, pp. 398-99.

103. *Ibid.*, p. 399. Cf. Oskar Seidlin, "Der Taugenichts ante portas," *op. cit.*, p. 14 ff.

104. *Op. cit.*, p. 385 ff.

105. *Ibid.*, p. 397.

106. *Ibid.*, especially on pp. 407-13.

107. *Ibid.*, p. 356.

108. *Ibid.*, pp. 413-16.

109. *Ibid.*, pp. 374-75.

110. *Ibid.*, p. 356.

111. *Ibid.*, p. 370.

112. *Ibid.*, pp. 417 ff.

113. *Ibid.*, p. 425. "Happy the man who stays in his house, sitting behind the stove and keeping his peace."

114. *Ibid.*, p. 434.

115. *Ibid.*, p. 416.

116. *Ibid.*, p. 433.

117. *Ibid.*, p. 434.

118. *Ibid.*, pp. 811 and 849.

119. *Ibid.*, p. 811.

120. *Ibid.*, p. 824.

121. *Ibid.*

122. *Ibid.*, p. 825.

123. *Ibid.*

124. *Ibid.*, p. 826.

125. *Ibid.*, p. 829.

126. *Ibid.*, p. 837.

127. *Ibid.*, p. 838.

128. *Ibid.*

129. *Ibid.*

130. *Ibid.*, p. 834.

131. *Ibid.* p. 839.

132. *Ibid.*, p. 842.

133. *Ibid.*, p. 849.

134. *Ibid.*, p. 823.

135. *Ibid.*, p. 824.

136. Cf. Chapter 2, p. 31

137. *Op. cit.*, pp. 834-35.

138. *Ibid.*, p. 836.

139. *Ibid.*

140. *Ibid.*

141. *Ibid.*, pp. 1102-04.

Chapter Five

1. For example, Alfons Perlick in his *Eichendorff und Nordrhein-Westfalen* (Veröffentlichungen der ostdeutschen Forschungsstelle im Land Nordrhein-Westfalen, Reihe A, Nr. 1/2 [Dortmund, 1960]) discusses the poet's acquaintance with a number of his contemporaries. There are many other studies about Eichendorff's personal relationships.

2. In his contribution to *Die deutsche Romantik: Poetik, Formen und Motive*, ed. Hans Steffen (Göttingen, 1967), entitled "Eichendorffs Wandel unter den Deutschen: Überlegungen zur Wirkungsgeschichte seiner Dichtung," Eberhard Lämmert examines the intellectual and emotional factors determining the character of Eichendorff's reception in Germany.

3. For example, the historical-critical edition started by August Sauer and Wilhelm Kosch, in *Sämtliche Werke des Freiherrn Joseph von Eichendorff* (Regensburg, 1908 ff).

4. See Chapter 4, pp. 131-32.

5. *Jacob Burckhardt und Eichendorff* (Freiburg: Albert-Verlag, 1960); also in: *Späte Studien* (Berne and Munich, 1964), pp. 276-343.

6. In addition to those mentioned, many other less known composers have set Eichendorff poems to music, for example K. Fr. Zelter, C. Bresger, H. Engel, Fr. Biebl, Fr. Glück, Fr. Th. Fröhlich, J. Bendig, Werner Josten, and Kurt Thomas.

7. Walther Killy, "Der Roman als romantisches Buch. Eichendorff: 'Ahnung und Gegenwart'," in *Wirklichkeit und Kunstcharakter* (Munich: Beck, 1963), pp. 36-58.

8. Oskar Seidlin, "Eichendorff und das Problem der Innerlichkeit," in *Festschrift für Bernhard Blume*, ed. Egon Schwarz *et al.* (Göttingen: Vandenhoeck & Ruprecht, 1967), pp. 126-145.

9. Cf. Werner Kohlschmidt, "Die symbolische Formelhaftigkeit von Eichendorffs Prosatil," in *Form und Innerlichkeit* (Berne, 1955), pp. 177-209.

10. Cf. T. S. Eliot, "What is Minor Poetry?" in *On Poetry and Poets* (New York: Farrar, Straus and Cudahy, 1957), pp. 34-51.

Selected Bibliography

1. MAJOR WORKS BY JOSEPH VON EICHENDORFF
   Ahnung und Gegenwart (1815)
   Das Marmorbild (1819)
   Krieg den Philistern (1824)
   Aus dem Leben eines Taugenichts (1826)
   Viel Lärmen um nichts (1832)
   Die Freier (1833)
   Dichter und ihre Gesellen (1834)
   Eine Meerfahrt (1835)
   Das Schloss Dürande (1837)
   Gedichte (1837)
   Die Entführung (1837)
   Die Glücksritter (1841)
   Geistliche Schauspiele von Calderon (translation, 1846-53)
   Libertas und ihre Freier (1849)
   Erlebtes (1857)
   Geschichte der poetischen Literatur Deutschlands (1857)
2. WORKS IN ENGLISH
   English translations of the work of Joseph von Eichendorff do not abound. A few are listed below.
   "Memoirs of a Good-For-Nothing." Tr. B. Q. Morgan. New York: Ungar, 1955.
   "The Happy-Go-Lucky or Leaves from the Life of a Good-for-Nothing." Tr. Mrs. A. L. Wister. Philadelphia and London: Lippincott, 1906; reprinted in *The German Classics: Masterpieces of German Romance*, ed. Frederick E. Pierce and Carl F. Schreiber. 1913. V, 238-323.
   The Marble Statue. Tr. F. E. Pierce, in *Fiction and Fantasy of German Romance*, ed. Frederick E. Pierce and Carl F. Schreiber. New York: Oxford University Press, 1927, pp. 131-70.

An Anthology of German Poetry from Hölderlin to Rilke in English, ed. Angel Flores. Gloucester, Mass.: Peter Smith, 1965, contains seventeen poems by Eichendorff.

3. EDITIONS

Sämtliche Werke des Freiherrn Joseph von Eichendorff. Historischkritische Ausgabe. Regensburg, 1908.

The historical-critical edition was begun by August Sauer and Wilhelm Kosch. Since 1958, Herman Kunisch and a staff of other scholars have been preparing and publishing the continuation of this work.

In addition to this edition, from which all the quotations in this book have been taken, the following edition can be recommended: *Joseph von Eichendorff: Neue Gesamtausgabe der Werke und Schriften in vier Bänden,* ed. Gerhard Baumann. Stuttgart, 1957-58; in 1960 a supplementary volume appeared.

Of the many separate editions of individual works by Eichendorff I shall only mention one, *Aus dem Leben eines Taugenichts,* ed. Egon Schwarz (with a *Nachwort,* a glossary, and a vocabulary). New York: McGraw-Hill, 1969.

This is the first American edition in the twentieth century, of Eichendorff's masterpiece.

4. BIBLIOGRAPHIES

In addition to the older compilation, Eichendorff, Karl Freiherr von, *Ein Jahrhundert Eichendorff-Literatur.* Regensburg, 1927, there is the "Eichendorff-Bibliographie" by Wolfgang Kron in *Eichendorff heute.* Munich: Bayerischer Schulbuch-Verlag, 1960, pp. 280-329 (which has 816 entries).

The standard bibliographies of German literature (Körner, Josef. *Bibliographisches Handbuch des deutschen Schrifttums.* Berne: Francke, 1949); and the volumes of Eppelsheimer-Köttelwesch, *Bibliographie der deutschen Literaturwissenschaft.* (Frankfurt T. Klostermann, which appeared from 1945 to date) contain long lists of Eichendorffiana.

Hock, Erich. "Neuere Eichendorff-Literatur," in *Wirkendes Wort* VIII (1958), 155-66.

Ranegger, Franz. "Die Eichendorff-Literatur seit 1945," in *Aurora,* No. 18 (1958) pp. 93-103, and *Aurora,* No. 19 (1959), pp. 93-98; Seidlin, Oskar. "1957: The Eichendorff-Year," in *The German Quarterly* XXXI (1958), 183-187; and Mauser, Wolfram. "Eichendorff-Literatur 1959-1962" in *Der Deutschunterricht* XIV (1962), 1-12, and "Eichendorff-Literatur 1962-1967" in *Der Deutschunterricht* (Beilage zu Heft 3/1968), are invaluable bibliographical aids to the Eichendorff scholar.

5. SOME EICHENDORFF STUDIES IN ENGLISH

Gillian, Rodger. "Eichendorff's Conception of the Supernatural World of the Ballad" in *German Life and Letters* (1959/60), 195-206.

Prawer, Siegbert S. *German Lyric Poetry, a Critical Analysis of Selected Poems from Klopstock to Rilke*. London, 1952.

Radner, Lawrence R. "Eichendorff's 'Marmorbild,' 'Götterdämmerung' and 'Deception'" in *Monatshefte* LII (1960), 183-88.

————. "The Instrument, the Musician, the Song: An Introduction to Eichendorff's Symbolism" in *Monatshefte* LVI (1964), 236-48.

Riley, Thomas A. "An Allegorical Interpretation of Eichendorff's *'Ahnung und Gegenwart'*" in *The Modern Language Review* LIV (1959), 204-13.

Schumann, Detlev W. "Some Scenic Motifs in Eichendorff's *Ahnung und Gegenwart*" in *JEGP* XVI (1957), 550-69.

Seidlin, Oskar. "Silesia in Southern Swabia [Wangen, Eichendorff Museum]" in *American German Review* XXI (1954/55), 7-9.

————. "1957, The Eichendorff Year" in *German Quarterly* XXXI (1958), 93-103.

————. "Eichendorff's Symbolic Landscape" in *PMLA* LXXII (1957), 465-61.

Workman, J. D. "The Significance of the Taugenichts for Eichendorffs in *Monatshefte* XXXIII (941), 64-76.

6. SOME WORKS ON EICHENDORFF IN GERMAN

The literature on Eichendorff is copious. Dozens of items have been collected by Wolfram Mauser since the publication of the Wolfgang Kron bibliography in 1960. Below is a select number of important and useful studies to be commented upon briefly.

Seidlin, Oskar. *Versuche über Eichendorff*. Göttingen: Vandenhoeck & Ruprecht, 1965. This book contains nine essays that add up to a coherent, subtle, and penetrating, sometimes esoteric, view of the poet. It may well be the most challenging study of Eichendorff in existence.

Eichendorff heute, ed. Paul Stöcklein. Munich: Bayerischer Schulbuch-Verlag, 1960. Seidlin is again represented in this collection of important (and sometimes not so important) essays, totaling fifteen in number, on the prose and poetry, the symbolism and personality, the relationship to society and to other writers, of our poet. I should like to single out the editor's own article on "Eichendorff's Persönlichkeit" as an illuminating analysis of the poet's mind and character, made with an awareness of modern methodological requirements (and of the renewed esteem bestowed upon biographical work). Another interesting contribution is Richard Alewyn's examination of the linguistic means through which Eichendorff creates the spacious landscapes peculiar to him. This work, entitled "Eine Landschaft Eichendorffs," has been dealt with at length in Chapter Two, pp. 60-62.

Spitzer, Leo. "Zu einer Landschaft Eichendorffs," in *Euphorion* LII (1958), pp. 142-52. Spitzer sheds additional light on the space problem by bringing to it his vast philological learning. His concept of "personification" comes close to my own view of Eichendorff's allegorical art.

Bollnow, Otto Friedrich. "Das romantische Weltbild bei Eichendorff" in *Unruhe und Geborgenheit im Weltbild neuerer Dichter.* (Stuttgart, 1953), pp. 227-59. The author is a philosopher, sensitive to literary values but accustomed to deal with essentials and, therefore, ready to dispense with estheticizing distractions. His study is perhaps the best short introduction to the work of Eichendorff known to me, even though few scholars will accept his classification of Eichendorff as a *Biedermeier* poet.

Requadt, Paul. "Eichendorffs Italien" in *Die Bildersprache der deutschen Italiendichtung* (Berne: A. Francke, 1962), pp. 107-25. Requadt's study is important because it places Eichendorff's (ambiguous) image of Italy into the concrete context of the entire German cult of Italy.

Mann, Thomas. *"Der Taugenichts" in Die neue Rundschau* XXVII, (1916), 1478-90; also in *Betrachtungen eines Unpolitischen* (Berlin, 1918), pp. 372-79. This interpretation of the Taugenichts as a prototype of the unpolitical German was discussed in Chapter Four, pp. 131-132. It is interesting because it marks a significant phase in Mann's own intellectual development. Since it also expresses something like the prevailing view of the novella and its author's artistic disposition at the time of its writing, it also serves to demonstrate the fundamental changes which the conception of Eichendorff has undergone.

Kunz, Josef. *Eichendorff. Höhepunkt und Krise der Spätromantik.* Oberursel, 1951. Kunz was one of the first to challenge the image of a carefree, ever-laughing Eichendorff and to point out the undercurrents of pessimism and ambivalences in his work, which he interprets as the expression of a crisis besetting German Romanticism in its late stages.

Rehm, Walther. "Jacob Burckhardt und Eichendorff" and "Prinz Rokoko im alten Garten: Eine Eichendorffstudie" in *Späte Studien.* (Berne and Munich: Francke, 1964), pp. 276-343 and 122-214 respectively. These essays are among the best works dealing with our poet. One is the study of an influence where one would not readily expect it, that of a Romantic poet on a great historian; the other goes to the core of Eichendorff's poetry, its involvement with history, the individual's as well as that of mankind.

Stöcklein, Paul. "Joseph von Eichendorff in *Die grossen Deutschen: Deutsche Biographie*, ed. H. Heimpel *et al.* (Berlin: Ullstein Verlag, 1956), III, 100-116. This is the best short biography of Eichendorff. My biographical chapter is profoundly indebted to the author's valuable insights.

Adorno, Theodor W. "Zum Gedächtnis Eichendorffs" in *Noten zur Literatur I.* (Frankfurt: Suhrkamp 1958), pp. 105-43. This is a curiously moving piece, the tribute paid by a Marxist and modern sociologist to a conservative poet of the German Romantic movement. It is thus an eloquent tribute to poetry itself.

Index